Transfigured

Transformational Fasting

RAENI BANKOLE

Transfigured

Transformational Fasting

RAENI BANKOLE

Dewalette Creations

This publication may not be reproduced, stored in a retrieval system, or transmitted in whole or in part, in any form or by any means, electronic, mechanical, photocopying, recording, or otherwise, without prior written permission of the publisher.

Transfigured - Transformational Fasting

Copyright © 2016 by Raeni Bankole
Paperback ISBN: 978-0-9862234-5-7

Published by Dewalette Creations
Phone: 630-481-6305
Email: info@dewalette.com
Website: www.dewalette.com

Unless otherwise stated all Bible references are taken from "The Holy Bible, New King James Version" ®. Copyright © 1982 by Thomas Nelson, Inc. Used by permission. All rights reserved.

Scripture quotations marked "KJV" are taken from the Holy Bible, King James Version, Cambridge, 1769.

Scriptures marked "NLT" are taken from the HOLY BIBLE, NEW LIVING TRANSLATION (NLT): Scripture quotations are taken from the Holy Bible, New Living Translation, copyright ©1996, 2004, 2007 by Tyndale House Foundation. Used by permission of Tyndale House Publishers, Inc., Carol Stream, Illinois 60188. All rights reserved.

Scriptures marked "AMP" are taken from the AMPLIFIED BIBLE (AMP): Scripture taken from the AMPLIFIED® BIBLE, Copyright © 1954, 1958, 1962, 1964, 1965, 1987 by the Lockman Foundation. Used by Permission.

Scripture taken from The Voice™. Copyright © 2008 by Ecclesia Bible Society. Used by permission. All rights reserved.

Printed in the United States of America

CONTENTS

Introduction 7
Day 1: Mountain of Transfiguration 19
Day 2: Open Heaven 26
Day 3: Ridiculous Miraculous 34
Day 4: Movers and Shakers 42
Day 5: Watchman Arise! 53
Day 6: Rain of Fire 62
Day 7: Day of Trumpets 74
Day 8: New Day New Name 85
Day 9: Power to Conceive 94
Day 10: Lion not a Dog 103
Day 11: Glory of God and Kings 111
Day 12: Destiny, Come Forth 119
Day 13: Electrified 126
Day 14: Double Perfection 135
Day 15: White as Light 142
Day 16: Alone with God 151
Day 17: Super-Human Strength 163
Day 18: World Changers 176
Day 19: Yoke Breakers 187
Day 20: Sons are Here 196
Day 21: Praise Storm 207
Conclusion: 216

INTRODUCTION

PLEASE DO NOT SKIP THIS IMPORTANT REVELATION!

The truth is that many dread fasting and so do not enjoy the benefit locked away in this spiritual exercise. You must be willing to endure the process in order for you to enjoy the benefits. Some people fast a lot but have not discovered the real power behind it. Fasting, like the word "fast" connotes, makes you swift like an eagle. It kills your flesh and silences its cravings and appetites so that the true you can emerge and live.

Like Paul wrote to the church in **Romans 8:13** admonishing us to mortify the flesh. What does it mean to mortify the flesh? It means to kill the flesh. The quickest way I know to kill the flesh is by depriving it of food and all that gratifies it. When you gain mastery in fasting and prayer, you will successfully master the flesh and grasp the secret that our Lord Jesus operated in when He walked the planet earth. Fasting empowers your spirit man and allows you to hear clearly from God. Fasting weakens the flesh (thus silencing the voice of the flesh) but strengthens the spirit man (thus amplifying the voice of the Spirit). The patriarchs of old who fasted and prayed with this understanding emerged as wonders to their generation.

If you engage this spiritual secret of fasting, you will emerge a walking wonder to your world like Moses, Elijah and our perfect example – Our Lord Jesus Christ.

FASTING: What does it mean?

Fasting is primarily an act of will – it is the abstinence from or reduction in the intake of food, drink, or both, for a period of time. It can be a partial fast or an absolute fast. It is not a religious obligation or rite of passage. Fasting brings empowerment for total transformation if done correctly according to scriptures. There two common types of fast: (1) Partial Fast and (2) Absolute Fast.

THE PARTIAL FAST:

A partial fast is the abstinence from certain types of food or drink – you may choose to abstain from food but continue to drink water. This may also be done by daily breaking with vegetables only like the Daniel's fast found in Daniel 1:8-10. It removes all types of sweets and indulgent food. Daniel repeated this type of fast again in Daniel 10. You can use your discretion for the specific hour on the prayer watch that you want to break your fast. My personal recommendation is that nursing mothers or pregnant women break at 12 noon because of the nourishment of their baby and their own overall health. I also encourage those with very busy work schedules to break at 3:00pm if they are engaging in an extended fast say 7 days, 14 days, 21 days, 40 days, 70 days and so on. This was recorded in scriptures as the time of the evening sacrifice in several places. One of which we can see when the Prophet Elijah called down fire in 1 Kings 18. Another example was when Daniel prayed in Daniel 9 and

10 and the angel appeared unto him. The length or duration of the fast is not as important as keeping the prayer watches – there are 8 watches in 24 hours. During the fast, you must observe the prayer watches by studying the word, praising the Lord and praying with fervency. You may choose to fast for a single day (24 hours), or for several days in a row. The most important thing is that you are led by the Holy Spirit through the fast regardless of the duration. This type of fast is very good when you are searching out a matter or trying to change your level spiritually.

This type of fast may be only partially restrictive, limiting particular foods or substances like bread, wine, coffee or sweets just as the patriarch Daniel did in Daniel 1, where he ate only vegetable and water with his three friends and they came out looking healthier than their peers after 10 days. I believe that they continued this fast till the end of their studies over the 3-year period according to **Daniel 1:8-20**.

> *8But Daniel purposed in his heart that he would not defile himself with the portion of the king's delicacies, nor with the wine which he drank; therefore he requested of the chief of the eunuchs that he might not defile himself. 9Now God had brought Daniel into the favor and goodwill of the chief of the eunuchs. 10And the chief of the eunuchs said to Daniel, "I fear my lord the king, who has appointed your food and drink. For why should he see your faces looking worse than the young men who are your age? Then you would endanger my head before the king." 11So Daniel said to the steward[a] whom the chief of the eunuchs had set over Daniel, Hananiah, Mishael, and Azariah, 12"Please test your servants for ten days, and let them give us vegetables to eat and water to drink. 13Then let our appearance be examined before you, and the appearance of the*

young men who eat the portion of the king's delicacies; and as you see fit, so deal with your servants." [14] So he consented with them in this matter, and tested them ten days. [15] And at the end of ten days their features appeared better and fatter in flesh than all the young men who ate the portion of the king's delicacies. [16] Thus the steward took away their portion of delicacies and the wine that they were to drink, and gave them vegetables. [17] As for these four young men, God gave them knowledge and skill in all literature and wisdom; and Daniel had understanding in all visions and dreams. [18] Now at the end of the days, when the king had said that they should be brought in, the chief of the eunuchs brought them in before Nebuchadnezzar. [19] Then the king interviewed[b] them, and among them all none was found like Daniel, Hananiah, Mishael, and Azariah; therefore they served before the king. [20] And in all matters of wisdom and understanding about which the king examined them, he found them ten times better than all the magicians and astrologers who were in all his realm.

The fast may also be intermittent in nature like one day every week. Some people usually like to start a new month with a fast or end the month with a fast. Fasting practices may preclude sexual intercourse and other activities as well as food. You need to devise what works for you as an individual and what works for your family as a whole. According to **1 Corinthians 7:3-5**, *Let the husband render to his wife the affection due her, and likewise also the wife to her husband. [4] The wife does not have authority over her own body, but the husband does. And likewise the husband does not have authority over his own body, but the wife does. [5] Do not deprive one another except with consent for a time, that you may give yourselves to fasting and prayer; and come together again so that Satan does not tempt you because of your lack of self-control.*

THE ABSOLUTE FAST:

You may adopt an absolute fast which is the complete abstinence from all food and liquid for a definite period of time – it is usually for a fewer number of days than the partial fast. The partial fast could extend for many days. Just like the apostle Paul in **Act 9:9** – he ate no food and drank no water for three whole days. This was also done by Esther and her uncle Mordecai who called for an absolute fast when they were faced with a death threat that could wipe out the entire Jewish race (**Esther 3 & 4**).

In **Esther 4:16**, Esther told her uncle, "Go, gather all the Jews who are present in Shushan, and fast for me; neither eat nor drink for three days, night or day. My maids and I will fast likewise. And so I will go to the king, which is against the law; and if I perish, I perish!"

The absolute fast is good at addressing issues with limited time associated with it. Like a death sentence or morbid diagnosis or a deadline of any sort. This type of fast overturns issues speedily because of the desperation involved. We all know what happened at the end of Esther's story: the adversary (Haman) was defeated and the Jews gained prominence in the land rather than experience complete annihilation that was originally planned against them. The truth was that the fast gave Esther uncommon boldness and unusual wisdom to tackle the adversary. The fast doesn't change God but it changes the individual engaging in it. When you fast, you are seeking God's face for unusual intelligence to deal with unusual situations.

I have personally experienced fasting for 3 days in a row abstaining from all food and I have discovered that it is much easier for me to round off an extended partial fast with an absolute fast. For example, when I fast for say 21 days or 40 days breaking every evening with food and water, my body would have adjusted tremendously to surviving with very little food. So then, it becomes easier to end the fast without food for 3 days in a row but I still take water as needed. I would strongly advise that for you to get the best out of an absolute fast, you may need to stay in-doors especially in the presence of the Lord. Look for a place of solitude to complete the fast to avoid distractions and avoid any unnecessary attention from people.

Fasting intensely will change you and destroy the flesh or what we call the carnal nature with its desires. I have never seen anyone who fasted with all intents and purposes (focusing on the Lord in prayer and meditation in the word) that has remained unchanged. The minute you engage this level of fasting, you will never be the same again. I want to also add that people who fast regularly do so because of the immediate effect and rewards of clarity they enjoy in the presence of the Lord. Fasting unclogs your spiritual channels and will allow you to hear and see into the spirit realm easily.

When I go on an extended fast, I make sure that my husband and I are on the same page because it becomes physically exerting to render due benevolence in the marriage at this time. But if it is just an intermittent fast, I am strengthened physically to perform my conjugal duties, the moment I break the fast. Please do not make this a rule of thumb – let the Lord lead you in your fasting journey. The truth is that when you make up your mind to minister to the Lord in a fast, things begin to align themselves in your favor. Your spouse may not even need you at that time and it is even better if you are both involved in the fast. Now, for those married to unbelieving spouses, you may need to attend to the needs of your spouse even during a fast because they have no clue about what you are doing spiritually. If there is a need, please by all means, meet it.

If you look through the Scriptures, you will see that there are some things that will not yield or leave without fasting accompanied with prayer - expelling demons is one of them. Jesus addressing His disciples when they could not heal a boy troubled by demonic spirits said in **Matthew 17:21**, "However, this kind does not go out except by prayer and fasting". In order for you to address some satanic afflictions and destroy the works of the flesh, you must be willing to fast and pray. Abstaining from food as a religious obligation without heartfelt prayers is tantamount to hunger strike – it is not productive and will yield no tangible result. In fact, it is destructive and can impact your physical health negatively.

There is an acceptable fast according to scriptures and my book the "CHOSEN FAST" addresses that topic exclusively. My prayer is that by the time you are through with this book, you will have gained a deeper understanding and obtained mastery for empowerment and the transformation that comes from fasting. Like our Lord Jesus mastered the flesh and defeated its nature completely, you will also defeat the carnal nature and the true you – the spiritual you – will emerge to your world!

GET READY FOR TRANSFORMATION!

If you follow the instructions in this prayer and fasting manual in accordance with scriptures, you will emerge as an amazement and a wonder to your world. Please fasten your seat belt because it promises to be a very exciting journey in the presence of the Father, Son and Holy Spirit. Get ready to be touched in places you have never been touched before. Are you going through a difficult situation? I sincerely believe that you will encounter the Almighty; who makes impossibility possible on this mountain. As much as I will like to encourage you to engage in a 21-day journey like I did, you do not have to go through the 21 days to experience the secrets I am sharing with you in this book.

Do not engage in an extended fast as a matter of religion nor to just follow the crowd. You can start small with a day, 3-days or even a week. Just make sure you are connecting to heaven through the word, prayer and praise. The ministry I am privileged to lead has a mandate to fast twice a year for 21 days – one is at the end of the year every December in preparation for the New Year. The second one is in the month of July which is significant because it is the 7th month. This allows us to harness every deliverable that is still outstanding for the second half of the year.

If you are determined to go through with an extended fast, please ask the Holy Spirit for help - that is the only sure way that you will not fail or faint. You can use this book as a daily devotional during a period of fasting and prayer. You may also use it for personal discovery i.e. searching through the pages of scriptures with or without a fast on a regular basis. This book may also serve as a tool for Bible study in a small group or a church. My prayer is that it will bless you tremendously. If you are blessed by a word, a page or the entire book, please pay it forward by sharing it with a loved one. You may buy them a copy or give them your own. Whatever you do, just make sure that you are spreading the Good News. Many personal testimonies have been recorded as a result of this 21-day fast – in my life, my family and the lives of the people in the Nehemiah Troop prayer ministry. Your testimony will be the next one in Jesus' name.

This book will help you take a closer and insightful look at what transpired on the Mountain of Transfiguration. Like I mentioned earlier, fasting empowers your spirit man and allows you to hear clearly from the Lord. When you fast, you will see into the spirit realm and hear the audible voice of the Lord just as it happened with Moses on Mount Sinai and Elijah in **1 Kings 19**. The same thing happened when our Lord Jesus went up the mountain to pray and the disciples gave the account that the heavens opened and the audible voice of the Father was heard saying, "This is my Beloved Son, hear him". Fasting will make you a wonder to your world like Moses, Elijah and our Lord Jesus Christ. All of these men were present on the "Mountain of Transfiguration" in Matthew 17. Notice that the transfiguration experience was written in three of the four Gospels – **Matthew 17, Mark 9** and **Luke 9**.

FASTING OPENS THE SPIRIT REALM TO YOU

Before you engage in any fast you must understand that it opens you up spiritually. When you fast, you are waiting on the Lord who is the Father of Spirits – He is the Foremost

Being in the ethereal (spirit) world. **John 4:24** states clearly that He is Spirit and all those who worship Him, must do so in spirit and in truth. The spirit realm is very real and whatever spiritual kingdom you expose yourself to, is the one that will influence you. Despite all the different religions and denominations out there today, there are only two spiritual kingdoms – the Kingdom of Light and the kingdom of darkness. The kingdom of Light is ruled by the Lord Jesus Christ the Son of God and that of darkness is ruled by Satan the devil. You either belong to one or the other.

The human race came from God (**Genesis 1:26-28**) but Satan tricked man into disobeying God and worshipping him (**Genesis 3**). Through the ages, God has been on the mission to reconcile man back to Himself. He sent His only begotten Son to die for our sins and He paid the full price for our disobedience redeeming us from every curse of the law according to **Colossians 2:15-16**. The Bible says for this purpose was the Son of God manifested, that He might destroy the works of the devil. He translated us from darkness into the Kingdom of His marvelous light. Jesus speaking in **John 14:6** said, I am the way, the truth and the life. No one comes to the Father except through Me. He is the only legitimate way into the spirit realm, any other way will lead you through illegitimate door that ends in the kingdom of darkness. If you are not sure where you truly belong I encourage you to make a decision right now before you open yourself up to the spirit realm.

You can become a part of God's Kingdom by accepting the finished work of His Son Jesus Christ on the Cross of Calvary about 2000 years ago. He died for you and rose again on the third day. He is now seated in heaven far above all principalities, powers, thrones and dominions in the visible and invisible realms. He has defeated the devil and He is calling on you to come to Him just as you are. He can transform the vilest sinner to the greatest saint. He can turn that mess into a message and use every detail of your story for His glory. You just need to let go of all the pain of your past by submitting your life to Him. You can take that burden and your struggle with sin to the foot of the Cross. You must leave the old man there with all his ways and put on the new man which is created after God in righteousness and true holiness. It is a miracle that happens when you confess Jesus as your Lord and Savior, renouncing Satan and the power of sin over you.

If you would like to become a new creation, then you can say this simple prayer out loud:

> *Lord Jesus, I accept you as my Lord and my Savior. Forgive me my sins. Wash me with your blood. Now, I know that I am born again to serve the living God. Amen*

WELCOME TO THE FAMILY OF GOD! You may now commence the journey of unending transformation and glorious discovery in His presence.

DAY 1

MOUNTAIN OF TRANSFIGURATION

On this first day of the fast, I would like to express that it is my personal opinion that Christ had been fasting for about a week or thereabout in the accounts given in the Gospel about His encounter on the Mountain of Transfiguration. If you look closely at the different scriptures in the book of Matthew, Mark and Luke, it says "After six days…" or "About eight days after these…" This connotes that He must have spent about a week fasting and praying to renew His strength after feeding the multitude. This simply means that whenever you experience a big breakthrough, it is not the time to start a feast on physical food. Rather, it is the time to begin feasting on spiritual meat so as to move to the next level of exploits in the Kingdom. Let us look at the account in **Matthew 17:1-3**:

> *Now after six days Jesus took Peter, James, and John his brother, led them up on a high mountain by themselves; and He was transfigured before them. His face shone like the sun, and His clothes became as white as the light. And behold, Moses and Elijah appeared to them, talking with Him.*

Fasting unveils your true nature to the world just like our Lord Jesus' experience – his face shone like the sun and His clothes became white as light. When you fast, your true nature as spirit shines forth and reveals who you truly are to the world. The outer cloak diminishes in form and appearance and your spiritual nature as "light" bursts forth.

Fasting also allows you to partake of the strong meat of the word (**Hebrews 5:14**); you begin to partake of solid food. When you deprive the flesh of physical bread, you must replace it with spiritual bread, which is the word of God. Jesus Christ said this in **Matthew 4:4** when He was fasting and was tempted by the devil, *"Man must not live by bread alone but by every word that proceeds out of the mouth of God."* The exact same scripture is reiterated in **Luke 4:4**.

WHAT MAKES YOU LIVE SUPERNATURALLY IS THE WORD OF GOD – it is spirit food! It is your spiritual bread!! It is what makes you carry weight in the spirit realm. Note that when they came down from the mountain in verse 14-21, the disciples could not heal a boy oppressed by a demon but Christ rebuked and cast the demon out effortlessly. He was empowered! His face was glowing with the effect of the encounter from the mountain top. When you fast, your face will glow too. Fasting will help you to shed physical weight so that you put on spiritual weight. Jesus was limitless and unstoppable! You can be the same way too if only you would learn to put off the flesh and his carnal nature. You destroy the 5 senses that limit your faith and you begin to operate by the sixth sense, walking effortlessly as a spirit. The popular verse of scripture in **Matthew 17:21** now comes to bear – *"this kind goes not out but by fasting and by prayer"*. What goes not out? The carnal nature; the defeated human nature; the doubt and unbelief; the fear and limitation that dwells in the flesh.

Fasting flushes out the carnal nature so that you can operate easily by the spirit.

Jesus attributed the disciples' inability to cast out the demon to unbelief – unbelief is a characteristic of the flesh. Please get this right now! Demons don't care if you fast or not. What they cannot stand is the power you gain through fasting and prayer. The power of faith – the ability to walk in the supernatural instead of the five senses. When you fast you kill the five senses (touch, smell, taste, sight and hearing) and you engage your sixth sense which is the spirit of faith. Now, when you speak by faith, you are guaranteed to have whatever you say according to **Mark 11:23-24**. DEMONS FEAR THAT!! When you fast and pray with in-depth study of the word, your faith increases "ginomously". Remember that faith comes by hearing and hearing by the word of God. Have you noticed that when you are drunk with the spirit of faith, you will be ready to face the devil and cut off his head if possible? Jesus lived in this state all his life and that was why demons tremble at his feet – He had faith without measure. You can grow in faith too and do the same as the Master on a daily basis.

As you will see throughout the pages of this book, the main text was taken from **Luke 9:28-43** (Please I encourage you to read it as you go through this book). The same scripture is confirmed in **Matthew 17:1-21** and **Mark 9:2-29**. Make sure you study the three different accounts for the purpose of understanding the effect fasting has on you as a believer. If you are baptized in the Holy Spirit with the evidence of speaking in tongues, I implore you to pray intensely in the Holy Ghost for at least an hour on the first day of this fast as you engage in uncommon praise. You will come to discover that your prayer may compel angelic attention but your praise draws the Father Himself. He inhabits the praises of His people (**Psalm 22:3**).

To get the best out of this fast, you must first make up your mind that it will be a fast like no other. The best place to start this extraordinary journey is in the word of God. Prayerfully meditate on the main scripture and as many others as you can find – take your own notes as much as possible because you will hear the Lord ministering to you audibly and/or with strong impressions in your heart. The eyes of your understanding will pop open because of this spiritual exercise. I strongly advice that you keep a dream or vision journal in the course of this fast, because not only will you hear with your spiritual ear and heart, but you will also see into the realm of the spirit just like our Lord and Master Jesus Christ. His earthly life was documented through the four Gospels just to show us how we ought to walk on planet earth because as He is, so are we in this world.

Please read the three renditions of the Mountain of Transfiguration experience in all three Gospels – Matthew 17:1-21, Mark 9:2-29 and Luke 9:28-43. Read it in different translations or versions if possible. I recommend the Amplified version, the New King James Version and the New Living Translation.

PRAYERFULLY STUDY AND MEDITATE: I suggest you read through and pray in tongues and read again and again till the scriptures open before your eyes.

See **LUKE 9:28-43**:

> *Now it came to pass, about eight days after these sayings, that He took Peter, John, and James and went up on the mountain to pray. As He prayed, the appearance of His face was altered, and His robe became white and glistening. And behold, two men talked with Him, who were Moses and Elijah, who appeared in glory and spoke of His decease which He was about to accomplish*

at Jerusalem. But Peter and those with him were heavy with sleep; and when they were fully awake, they saw His glory and the two men who stood with Him. Then it happened, as they were parting from Him, that Peter said to Jesus, "Master, it is good for us to be here; and let us make three tabernacles: one for You, one for Moses, and one for Elijah"—not knowing what he said. While he was saying this, a cloud came and overshadowed them; and they were fearful as they entered the cloud. And a voice came out of the cloud, saying, "This is My beloved Son. Hear Him!" When the voice had ceased, Jesus was found alone. But they kept quiet, and told no one in those days any of the things they had seen. Now it happened on the next day, when they had come down from the mountain, that a great multitude met Him. Suddenly a man from the multitude cried out, saying, "Teacher, I implore You, look on my son, for he is my only child. And behold, a spirit seizes him, and he suddenly cries out; it convulses him so that he foams at the mouth; and it departs from him with great difficulty, bruising him. So I implored Your disciples to cast it out, but they could not." Then Jesus answered and said, "O faithless and perverse generation, how long shall I be with you and bear with you? Bring your son here." And as he was still coming, the demon threw him down and convulsed him. Then Jesus rebuked the unclean spirit, healed the child, and gave him back to his father. And they were all amazed at the majesty of God. But while everyone marveled at all the things which Jesus did, He said to His disciples.

It is time to pray.

DAY 1 PRAYER POINTS

1. Thank You Lord for my own appointment with destiny on this Mountain of Transfiguration. Thank You for being such a God of grace and love! Thank You for abundant revelation!

2. Thank You Lord for bringing me to this fast so I can enter my season of perfection and rest round about. Thank You for life and the vibrant breath in me.

3. Thank You Lord for translating me from darkness to light and for defeating every attack of the enemy against me and my entire household. Thank You for the blood of Jesus atoning, protecting and renewing me.

4. Thank You Lord for going ahead of me and giving me the revelation into your perfect will for my life. I am excited about my journey in Christ Jesus my Lord!

5. Father Lord, I receive a fresh baptism of praise and worship; I enter into a covenant of gratitude and unusual praise like your servant David.

6. Lord, from today, I put on the garment of praise and I receive a fresh oil of gladness that makes me stand out among my peers. I operate with distinction and grace in Jesus' name

7. I declare Your praise like the Psalmist – morning afternoon and night. I am supernaturally enabled to observe all the prayer watches regardless of my schedule in Jesus' name.

8. Lord, show me the secrets of praise warfare and grant me access to the realms of supernatural exploits like Paul and Silas, Jehoshaphat and the multiplying effect of praise like my Lord Jesus Christ who fed multitudes.

9. Father Lord, I offer succeeding praise for all you have done for me and my loved ones this year! MENTION them one by one – graduation, weddings, new job, new home, new car, good health, safety and near misses, broken relationships and unbroken relationships, newborns, new friends and so on.

10. Father Lord, I offer preceding praise for the things that are waiting to manifest into the physical according to your divine time. Nothing missing, nothing broken! Blessings without sorrow and perfect peace -- mention those expectations with thanksgiving. PERFECT PRAISE PRODUCES PERFECT PEACE!

Philippians 4:6-7 Be anxious for nothing, but in everything by prayer and supplication, with thanksgiving, let your requests be made known to God; and the peace of God, which surpasses all understanding, will guard your hearts and minds through Christ Jesus.

11. Father Lord, I thank You in advance for the encounter I have from this mountain. Multitudes will gather to see your glory in my life just like Jesus when He came down from the Mountain of Transfiguration. I am transformed to transform my world in Jesus mighty name!

12. COMMUNION: Father, I receive uncommon grace from the blood of Jesus to go on this 21-day journey of transformation; I declare it is not by power and not by might but by your spirit O Lord! I shout grace, grace to the Capstone. I am a completer; I am a finisher in Jesus' name!

Give thanks for answered prayers.

INSTRUCTION: At the midnight watch, ask the Lord to show you the secret key of prayer and fasting that opens the spirit realm.

DAY 2

OPEN HEAVEN

On this second day, I know of a fact that your life cannot be the same again because you have come to tap into the ultimate power source of the entire universe. You have come to touch the real live wire and the highest voltage power HIMSELF – you have been called out of darkness as the light of the world. The topic today is OPEN HEAVEN. I hope you have read all the three accounts of the Gospel where the Mountain of Transfiguration was recorded in scriptures as instructed?

Let us take a look at **Luke 9:29-37** in the Amplified version.

> *And as He was praying, the appearance of His countenance became altered different, and His raiment became dazzling white flashing with the brilliance of lightning. And behold, two men were conversing with Him—Moses and Elijah, Who appeared in splendor and majesty and brightness and were speaking of His exit from life, which He was about to bring to realization at Jerusalem. Now Peter and those with him were weighed down with sleep, but when they fully awoke, they saw His glory splendor and majesty and brightness and the two men who stood with Him. And it occurred as the men were parting from Him that Peter said to Jesus, Master, it is delightful and good that we are*

here; and let us construct three booths or huts—one for You and one for Moses and one for Elijah! not noticing or knowing what he was saying. But even as he was saying this, a cloud came and began to overshadow them, and they were seized with alarm and struck with fear as they entered into the cloud. Then there came a voice out of the cloud, saying, This is My Son, My Chosen One or My Beloved; listen to and yield to and obey Him! And when the voice had died away, Jesus was found there alone. And they kept still, and told no one at that time any of these things that they had seen. Now it occurred the next day, when they had come down from the mountain, that a great multitude met Him.

I declare that after you complete these 21 days fast and come down from this Mountain of Transfiguration, you will begin to draw the attention of multitudes like the Master Himself. Your voice will compel demons to come trembling out of their closed places. Heaven will open over your head for supernatural exploits and unlimited provision. You will begin to know things before they happen. You will hear God's voice openly and clearly on a daily basis and experience visions and revelations of heaven like never before.

If you notice in the above scripture, heaven opened and they heard God speak with clarity. What happened was that Jesus took Peter, James and John up there to see what happens every time He snuck off to pray by Himself. He had the habit of observing the prayer watches. It was recorded in scriptures that He got up early in the morning, way before everyone was awake to pray. He must have also observed the midday (12 Noon) or 3pm watch many times because the disciples saw him praying in **Matthew 6** and **John 11**. And they asked him to teach them how to pray. He must have observed the midnight watch too because the Bible records many times that he will go away by himself to pray and give the Father feedback about His many assignments. Just like he did after feeding the multitude in the scriptures we read in **Matthew 17** and **Luke 9**.

Many Christians dread fasting because they do not know of the benefits involved in this spiritual exercise. Fasting OPENS YOUR HEAVEN – IT WILL ALLOW YOU TO HEAR GOD WITHOUT ANY DISTRACTION FROM THE FLESH OR THE ENEMY. Many are so afraid to go without food not knowing that the pleasures that earthly food brings is nothing to be compared with the power and enjoyment that spiritual food brings. Jesus, speaking in Matthew 4:4 when he was fasting and the devil told him to change the stone to bread, that man must not live by bread alone but by every word that proceeds out of the mouth of the living God. His word is the food for your spirit and soul. Your physical body can also benefit exceedingly from this spiritual food. Not only will it keep excess weight off but it will renew your physical strength and keep sickness at bay. Fasting unveils your true nature to the world.

Notice that on the Mountain of Transfiguration, Jesus' face shone as flashes of lightning. So also will you shine and dazzle when you begin to partake of strong meat in the word of God as you fast. When you deprive the flesh of physical bread and replace it with spiritual food (the word of God), you will increase in wisdom and spiritual stature, waxing strong in the spirit. That is the true meaning of the scripture in Matthew 4:4 that says, "Man must not live by bread alone but by every word that proceeds out of the mouth of God."

When you fast, you mortify or kill the flesh with all the lust thereof. That was why Paul said in **Acts 24:16**,

> *"Therefore I always exercise and discipline myself mortifying my body, deadening my carnal affections, bodily appetites,*

and worldly desires, endeavoring in all respects to have a clear unshaken, blameless conscience, void of offense toward God and toward men."

Some Christians cannot grow past where they are right now because of the inability to conquer the belly god. They find it hard to defeat the control and cravings of the flesh. Don't get me wrong, initially, when you first start fasting, your body will rebel. It will cry, mourn, growl and groan but please hang in there and endure the process so as to enjoy the benefits in full as you grow in grace. The reason why many also say they have fasted a lot but have no results to show is because they are yet to discover the real truth about fasting and praying.

My word of caution to you is this: if you fast without praying or feeding on the word, you have just wasted a good meal and your precious time. Fasting transforms you into a new being just like Jesus' experienced on the Mount of Transfiguration. Fasting like the word *fast* connotes will make you swift like an eagle. It will kill your flesh and silence its cravings and appetite so that the true you can emerge and live. Fasting empowers your spirit man and allows you to hear clearly from God about any subject matter and most especially about your assignment per time on the earth. For example, our Lord Jesus went to the Mountain of Transfiguration to get the detailed information about His exit from the earth. You can do the same by seeking God's face about every detail of your assignment on the earth. Nothing should catch you by surprise.

FASTING EMPOWERS YOU SUPERNATURALLY!

Remember Elijah went in the strength of the angels' food he ate for 40 days. So also the children of Israel were not feeble when they ate the spiritual food called manna in the wilderness that rained down from the Lord. When you are fasting without studying the word of God, you will just end up very cranky because your belly is empty and your physical brain is starved of fuel as well. It is just hunger strike and it adds no value whatsoever to the **"fastee"**. But when you do it according to the word of God, laboring in the word, prayer and praise, then you will emerge a transformer like Moses, Elijah and Jesus. The meat of the word that you start feasting on represents your own manna from the Lord. It is your spiritual food. It grows and nurtures your spirit man, resulting in supernatural development.

Did you also notice that Moses and Elijah were the two men on the Mountain of Transfiguration with our Lord Jesus Christ? It was not a coincidence at all. These two men were patriarchs who exemplified rigorous fasting and fervent prayer in their lifetime. Their lives and ministry was filled with supernatural exploits and unusual strength. Elijah called down fire and rain in **1 Kings 18** and he physically outran the chariot of a king and beat him on a race while he ran on foot. Can you imagine someone running ahead of a royal vehicle on foot? Remember, it was the chariot of a king we are talking about here, so it we can compare his vehicle to the very best cars of today, say a Bentley or Range Rover. I truly believe that it was his manner to fast regularly because afterwards, it was recorded in **1 Kings 19** that he fasted for 40 days without food or water. This man was such an empowered transformer that he called down fire and lighting everywhere he went. He finally departed the scene on planet earth on a chariot of fire. Imagine flying on a fiery jet! What an exit! What a thrill!! You can operate with the same anointing of fire today.

Same with the man Moses, he was a regular mountain dweller. He had mastered the act of shutting out the noise and walking away from the crowd. He wrote the first five books of the Bible. He spoke to God face to face, according to **Numbers 12:6-8**. He saw the glory of the Lord not by eating chicken burger like the rest of the people. He abstained from physical food for a season at a time to be sustained by the meat of the presence of the Most High. Fasting will make you a wonder to your world like Moses, Elijah and Jesus all mentioned in **Matthew 17**. Notice that the Mountain of Transfiguration mentioned also all three of them together at the same time.

See **Matthew 17:1-3** *"Now after six days Jesus took Peter, James, and John his brother, led them up on a high mountain by themselves; and He was transfigured before them. His face shone like the sun, and His clothes became as white as the light. And behold, Moses and Elijah appeared to them, talking with Him."*

As an individual, do you want to experience open heaven on a daily basis? Do you want to see day and night visions? Do you want to hear the Father with clarity and commune with heaven on a regular basis? Do you want demons to bow down crying before you? Do you want to live a life of perpetual faith? Then you must lay aside the weight and sin that so easily besets, according to **Hebrews 12:1**, *Therefore we also, since we are surrounded by so great a cloud of witnesses, let us lay aside every weight, and the sin which so easily ensnares us, and let us run with endurance the race that is set before us.*

You must learn to turn on the switch of the spirit through fasting and prayer. You must gain mastery in unlocking your spiritual blessings through the keys of the kingdom of which fasting and prayer are individual keys. These 21 days will turn you around such that you will compel the attention of the world for His glory in Jesus' name.

It is time to pray!

DAY 2 PRAYER POINTS

1. Thank You Lord for touching me with your power and grace. Thank You for this second day of revival and supernatural revelation of your glory. Thank You for enabling grace to continue this fast.

2. Thank You for showing me the secret of fasting. Thank You for opening the eyes of my understanding and granting me the spirit of wisdom and revelation in the knowledge of you.

3. Thank You for the divine exchange on the cross of Calvary letting Christ die for my sins and giving me His eternal life and everlasting forgiveness from all sins.

4. Father Lord, enable me to maximize this season of fasting laboring in the word, prayer and uncommon praise. Grant me access into your secret place and open my eyes to see visions of heaven in Jesus name.

5. Father Lord, empower me to command the attention of the multitude for your glory and make my voice a terror to the kingdom of darkness. Let the strangers (spirit of afflictions, oppressions and demonic possessions) begin to come trembling out of their closed places in Jesus name.

6. Father, open the heavens over my head and move me into the realm of supernatural exploits and unlimited provisions in Jesus name. Open my eyes to see the invisible and open my ears to hear the inaudible in Jesus mighty name.

7. As I watch on this tower and wait on this mountain, show me things to come. Let me know of things before they happen in my family, city, nation and generation in Jesus name.

8. Lord, grant me the grace to fast and pray until I gain speed and obtain surpassing strength like Moses, Elijah and my Master Jesus. My vision will not grow dim nor my strength diminish in Jesus name.

9. Father, show me the secrets locked away in the remaining months of this year. Help me to operate by divine agenda and empower me to run with divine timing in the name of Jesus.

10. COMMUNION: As I eat this bread and drink this cup, give me a heartwarming experience with you like in **Luke 24:30-32**. Let my eyes of understanding be opened to know who I am in you and what you sent me here to accomplish in Jesus name.

Give thanks for answered prayer.

INSTRUCTION: Pray for 30 minutes at the midnight watch or the early watch at 3am to address long-standing issues.

DAY 3

RIDICULOUS MIRACULOUS

Today is the third day of the fast and the Bible says in **Hosea 6:2**, *"After two days He will revive us; on the third day He will raise us up that we may live before Him."* Today, the Lord will raise you up! Far above that situation and any strange battle. He will lift your head above all the raging of the enemy of your father's house or your mother's house. **Psalm 27:6** says,

> *Now my head shall be lifted up above my enemies all around me; Therefore I will offer sacrifices of joy in His tabernacle; I will sing, yes, I will sing praises to the Lord.*

The topic for today is the RIDICULOUS MIRACULOUS. What does ridiculous mean? It means something laughable or worthy of ridicule or derision. Who is the subject of our ridicule today? – The devil and his cohorts, evil personalities, spirit of affliction, stagnation and ungodly delay. Remember the Lord said in **Psalm 2:4**,

> *"He who sits in the heavens shall laugh; The Lord shall hold them in derision.*

It is your season of laughter and permanent victory. Never again will you be afraid of any attack of the enemy; instead it will bring amusement and laughter to you. From today, you will laugh the enemy to scorn. Why? Because you have what it takes! All power and authority belongs to our King and He has bestowed the same to you and I. He manifested this unusual authority when He walked the earth according to scriptures.

As you make progress in this fast, the Lord will make you an astonishment and an amazement to your world. What used to be impossible for you before this fast will become a walk over for you in Jesus' name. As you pray and fast from today, you will contact the power that will make demons bow and tremble before you. As you command them out of their strongholds and closed places, they will obey you like it was said in **Psalm 18:44-45**, As soon as they heard of me, they obeyed me; foreigners (strangers) submitted themselves cringingly and yielded feigned obedience to me. Foreigners (strangers) lost heart and came trembling out of their caves or strongholds. You will be a walking TRANSFORMER conducting raw power from the Source. You will display the majesty and magnificence of our King.

Notice what the scripture says in **Mark 9:15**,

> *"And immediately all the crowd, when they saw Jesus returning from the holy mount, His face and person yet glistening, they were greatly amazed and ran up to Him and greeted Him."*

His face was still glowing with the power. That power compelled people to come to him. You will compel the world to our King as you make a ridicule of difficult and challenging situations in Jesus' name. The man cried out because his only child was being molested by the devil and Jesus cheaply made a ridicule of him. From today, you will begin to solve uncommon problems at work and your school. You will be empowered to address strange afflictions like cancer, heart problems, kidney problems and other incurable disease with ease. Through your light, many will be delivered from the dungeon of affliction in Jesus' name.

Like I mentioned before, Moses and Elijah were present on the Mountain of Transfiguration with Jesus for a reason. They were men who spent time in the presence of the Lord, fasting and praying. They were a shadow or type of the things to come. Moses also came down from the mountain with a glowing face like Jesus and Elijah exited on a chariot of fire just like our Lord went up on the cloud back to the Father of glory.

Exodus 34:29-30,

> *Now it was so, when Moses came down from Mount Sinai (and the two tablets of the Testimony were in Moses' hand when he came down from the mountain), that Moses did not know that the skin of his face shone while he talked with Him. So when Aaron and all the children of Israel saw Moses, behold, the skin of his face shone, and they were afraid to come near him.*

DIFFERENCE BETWEEN LAW AND GRACE

Moses' face made the people afraid because he was holding onto the law (which pricked the conscience and condemned sinners) but Christ on the other hand was full of mercy and grace that it pulled the crowd toward Him. That is the difference. One thing I want us to know though, is that when you spend time in the presence of the Lord, it will show on your face. The glory of Moses' face was so bright that he had to cover his face whenever he came out of God's presence to meet with people. If people could see the light, what do you think of the devil and his cohorts? They will be blinded by it!

Exodus 34:34-35,

But whenever Moses went in before the Lord to speak with Him, he would take the veil off until he came out; and he would come out and speak to the children of Israel whatever he had been commanded. And whenever the children of Israel saw the face of Moses, that the skin of Moses' face shone, then Moses would put the veil on his face again, until he went in to speak with Him.

Now the Bible makes it clear that everything in the Old Testament is only a shadow of the new covenant.

2 Corinthians 3:7-8,

But if the ministry of death, written and engraved on stones, was glorious, so that the children of Israel could not look steadily at the face of Moses because of the glory of his countenance, which glory was passing away, how will the ministry of the Spirit not be more glorious?

You are living under a new dispensation because Jesus already died for our sins. Therefore, your light should attract men to the Lord and not turn them away. You will draw many to the King of Kings through His unfailing love. Your light draws men to God but terrifies devils and demons. You have a more glorious power than Moses because of Jesus. The power that cannot be insulted by the forces of darkness! The power that ridicules the devil. You possess the anointing to operate in the miraculous on a daily basis. You are ridiculous to the logical mind! You are a miraculous wonder to your generation changing from one level of glory to another according to **2 Corinthians 3:13-18**,

...unlike Moses, who put a veil over his face so that the children of Israel could not look steadily at the end of what was passing away. But their minds were blinded. For until this day the same

> *veil remains unlifted in the reading of the Old Testament, because the veil is taken away in Christ. But even to this day, when Moses is read, a veil lies on their heart. Nevertheless when one turns to the Lord, the veil is taken away. Now the Lord is the Spirit; and where the Spirit of the Lord is, there is liberty. But we all, with unveiled face, beholding as in a mirror the glory of the Lord, are being transformed into the same image from glory to glory, just as by the Spirit of the Lord.*

Every glory that was covered and veiled in the Old Testament is now openly revealed through our Lord Jesus Christ. What a privilege to be living in a time such as this!! This means the darker the season, the brighter your light should shine. Someone should notice something about you at work. Your light must touch someone from today!

I love this scripture so much because it says we are TRANSFORMED from one intensity of glory to another as we focus on Him! Please do not let anything distract you from this 21 days journey and I assure you, you will emerge a wonder to your world.

Take a look at the man Elijah, the prophet of fire who had contacted so much power from the source that he was literally spitting fire and lightning at will. **2 Kings 2:9-11** says,

> *And so it was, when they had crossed over, that Elijah said to Elisha, "Ask! What may I do for you, before I am taken away from you?" Elisha said, "Please let a double portion of your spirit be upon me." So he said, "You have asked a hard thing. Nevertheless, if you see me when I am taken from you, it shall be so for you; but if not, it shall not be so." Then it happened, as they continued on and talked, that suddenly a chariot of fire appeared with horses of fire, and separated the two of them; and Elijah went up by a whirlwind into heaven.*

You can also ask for a double anointing of Jesus today and it is very scriptural because Jesus himself said that anyone who believes in His name will do greater works. Elisha performed exactly double of the miracles that Elijah did. Immediately after he was imparted with the same anointing, he began to walk in the realm of the miraculous.

2 Kings 2:12-15,

> *And Elisha saw it, and he cried out, "My father, my father, the chariot of Israel and its horsemen!" So he saw him no more. And he took hold of his own clothes and tore them into two pieces. He also took up the mantle of Elijah that had fallen from him, and went back and stood by the bank of the Jordan. Then he took the mantle of Elijah that had fallen from him, and struck the water, and said, "Where is the Lord God of Elijah?" And when he also had struck the water, it was divided this way and that; and Elisha crossed over. Now when the sons of the prophets who were from Jericho saw him, they said, "The spirit of Elijah rests on Elisha." And they came to meet him, and bowed to the ground before him.*

I declare that those situations that used to ridicule you will begin to bow before you in the mighty name of Jesus. That exam that has made a mockery at you will bow to this power you will contact on this mountain in Jesus' name. That strange affliction will bow out trembling in Jesus' name.

Proverbs 14:19,

> *"The evil will bow before the good, And the wicked at the gates of the righteous."*

From today evil will begin to bow before you as you contact the limitless God! Incurable sickness like cancer will bow at your gate. Poverty will bow at your gate. Failure will give up at your gate in Jesus mighty name! At work and in your school, those who never paid attention to you will begin to reckon with you as the word of the Lord says in **Isaiah 49:23**,

> *"Kings shall be your foster fathers, And their queens your nursing mothers; They shall bow down to you with their faces to the earth, And lick up the dust of your feet. Then you will know that I am the Lord, For they shall not be ashamed who wait for Me."*

It is time to pray!

DAY 3 PRAYER POINTS

1. Thank You Lord for the Mountain of Transfiguration! Thank You for counting me worthy to be called Your own through the blood of Jesus.

2. Thank You Lord for the sustaining grace to continue on this 21 days fasting and prayer. Thank You for daily renewing me.

3. Thank You Father for giving me insight into Your divine secrets and revealing to me things that were hidden away before the foundation of the world.

4. Father Lord, I renounce every sin and denounce every covenant that I entered into (knowingly or unknowingly) that has made mockery of the anointing over my life. I plead the blood of Jesus and declare total liberty from _____ (mention the affliction).

5. From today, baptize me with the fire of the Holy Ghost and with power that cannot be insulted in Jesus' name. Let the strangers come trembling out of their strongholds by fire and by force.

6. Father Lord, let Your anointing show in my life. Let Your power show in my health, finances, academics, marriage, career and ministry. Empower me to walk in the ridiculous miraculous - humiliating failure, barrenness, disease, stagnation and every satanic barrier in Jesus' name.

7. Father Lord, I crave Your presence in my life like never before and I desire the intimacy that Jesus had with You in prayer on the earth; let my prayer life move from ordinary to extra-ordinary in Jesus' name.

8. Lord, let Your power on my life attract people with the Holy Spirit conviction that brings permanent change. Make me an effective change agent – transforming my generation for righteousness.

9. From today, I begin to operate with the anointing that is relevant in the workplace and my secular sphere of influence. I will be a resource-center and a power-house to the lost and brokenhearted in Jesus' name. I am PROBLEM SOLVER to my generation!

10. COMMUNION: Lord, anoint me for the miraculous and empower me to make ridicule out of demonic afflictions in the lives of people. Make me a gate-keeper of peace and restoration for the oppressed in Jesus' mighty name.

Acts 10:38, *How God anointed Jesus of Nazareth with the Holy Spirit and with power, who went about doing good and healing all who were oppressed by the devil, for God was with Him.*

Give thanks for answered prayer.

INSTRUCTION: READ and PRAY with **Psalm 18:1-end** with fervent praise at the midnight watch or early morning watch at 3am.

DAY 4

MOVERS AND SHAKERS

Today is the fourth day of the fast. In **Genesis 1:16-19**, God made two great lights,

> ...*the greater light to rule the day, and the lesser light to rule the night. He made the stars also. God set them in the firmament of the heavens to give light on the earth, and to rule over the day and over the night, and to divide the light from the darkness. And God saw that it was good. So the evening and the morning were the fourth day.*

From today, as a great light you will begin rule over all affairs of darkness with mastery. You will shine as a star in all areas of your endeavors and as you contact power in the night watches to win battles, you will begin to command your day before they emerge in Jesus' name!

Today, we will look into what I call MOVERS AND SHAKERS. Who are the shakers and movers? The sons of the Most High who move things in prayer and shake up the earth in praise. Our Father is the Immovable Mover and Unshakeable Shaker. Remember how He showed up for Paul and Silas in **Acts 16:25-26**:

> *But at midnight Paul and Silas were praying and singing hymns to God, and the prisoners were listening to them. Suddenly there was a great earthquake, so that the foundations of the prison were shaken; and immediately all the doors were opened and everyone's chains were loosed.*

You can compel the presence of God down through praise and when He shows up, His entourage shows up with sounds of thunder, earthquake and lightning as their siren just like in **Exodus 19:16-20**:

> *Then it came to pass on the third day, in the morning, that there were thunderings and lightnings, and a thick cloud on the mountain; and the sound of the trumpet was very loud, so that all the people who were in the camp trembled. And Moses brought the people out of the camp to meet with God, and they stood at the foot of the mountain. Now Mount Sinai was completely in smoke, because the Lord descended upon it in fire. Its smoke ascended like the smoke of a furnace, and the whole mountain quaked greatly. And when the blast of the trumpet sounded long and became louder and louder, Moses spoke, and God answered him by voice. Then the Lord came down upon Mount Sinai, on the top of the mountain. And the Lord called Moses to the top of the mountain, and Moses went up.*

You can see that the same occurred on the Mountain of Transfiguration as Jesus prayed, the heavens opened **Luke 9:29**:

> *And as He was praying, the appearance of His countenance became altered different, and His raiment became dazzling white flashing with the brilliance of lightning.*

Verse 34 says,

> *But even as he was saying this, a cloud came and began to*

overshadow them, and they were seized with alarm and struck with fear as they entered into the cloud.

Please stop approaching your prayer casually from today; go before the Lord with an expectation to encounter the invisible and hear the inaudible.

Stop praising God absent-mindedly but with all your faculties present – spirit, soul and body and you will be surprised how you will move heaven into your space. God inhabits the praises of HIS PEOPLE and He said in that day, if you seek me with all of your heart, you will find me (**Jeremiah 29:13**)

As a mover and a shaker, I want to encourage you to take advantage of the prayer watches like our Master Jesus. Many times the Bible mentioned that he went away by himself to pray at odd hours of the night.

Matthew 14:23,

And after He had dismissed the multitudes, He went up into the hills by Himself to pray.

He was there alone. And in the fourth watch between 3:00 - 6:00 a.m. of the night, Jesus came to them, walking on the sea. (vs. 25). He must have prayed through the evening watch to the fourth watch. The evening watch starts at 6pm, the second watch is 9pm, the third watch of the night is at midnight (12am) and the fourth watch at 3am. Go and study the gospels, you will see that Jesus observed the prayer watches all through His ministry on the earth and we know He shook the world. The disciples followed this example too in **Acts 3:1**; Peter and John were going up to the temple at the hour of prayer, the ninth hour (three o'clock in the afternoon), when they encountered the crippled man and healed him and we know the rest of the story.

There are 8 prayer watches in 24 hours - starting at 12 midnight when a new day begins, 3am, 6am, 9am, 12noon, 3pm, 6pm and 9pm. A new watch starts again at midnight. No wonder Paul and Silas brought on an earthquake at midnight. The midnight hour is so crucial because the old day hands over to a new one at 12 midnight, an old month hands over to a new one at midnight, an old year hands over to a new year at 12 midnight. Power changes hands at midnight, a shift occurs at midnight. The psalmist talked about the night watches in

Psalm 63:6,

When I remember You upon my bed and meditate on You in the night watches.

Psalm 119:62 also says,

At midnight I will rise to give thanks to You, Because of Your righteous judgments.

Psalm 119:148 also confirms the night watches:

My eyes anticipate the night watches and I am awake before the cry of the watchman, that I may meditate on Your word.

You must learn to pray, meditate and praise the Lord at this crucial hour. As a mover and a shaker, you must gain mastery of this important hour in spiritual warfare. Some battles can only be addressed effectively at night because they were planted by the enemy at night.

Matthew 13:25,

But while men slept, his enemy came and sowed tares among the wheat and went his way.

Psalm 22:2 talks about the midnight cry; you must not be silent at midnight calling out for intervention for your case and interceding for others. Jesus' teaching about prayer and interceding in **Luke 11:5-10** says,

> *"Which of you shall have a friend, and go to him at midnight and say to him, 'Friend, lend me three loaves; for a friend of mine has come to me on his journey, and I have nothing to set before him'; and he will answer from within and say, 'Do not trouble me; the door is now shut, and my children are with me in bed; I cannot rise and give to you'? I say to you, though he will not rise and give to him because he is his friend, yet because of his persistence he will rise and give him as many as he needs. "So I say to you, ask, and it will be given to you; seek, and you will find; knock, and it will be opened to you. For everyone who asks receives, and he who seeks finds, and to him who knocks it will be opened.*

Some household wickedness and evil altars can only be dismantled at night. See how Gideon was instructed by the Lord to destroy the evil altars of his fathers house in **Judges 6:25-27,**

> *Now it came to pass the same night that the Lord said to him, "Take your father's young bull, the second bull of seven years old, and tear down the altar of Baal that your father has, and cut down the wooden image that is beside it; and build an altar to the Lord your God on top of this rock in the proper arrangement, and take the second bull and offer a burnt sacrifice with the wood of the image which you shall cut down." So Gideon took ten men from among his servants and did as the Lord had said to him. But because he feared his father's household and the men of the city too much to do it by day, he did it by night.*

MIRACLES HAPPEN AT MIDNIGHT:

Midnight is a strategic hour in the spirit. You must learn to lay low and pick up your battle-axe at midnight. Like Samson, you may need to go to the ancient gates by midnight and totally uproot that force that will not allow you to get married! Samson pulled out the gates of resistance at midnight. See **Judges 16:3**,

> *And Samson lay low till midnight; then he arose at midnight, took hold of the doors of the gate of the city and the two gateposts, pulled them up, bar and all, put them on his shoulders, and carried them to the top of the hill that faces Hebron.*

Ruth's marital destiny was revisited at midnight (see Ruth 3:8 in your spare time). In **Acts 20:7**, the resurrection of Euthycus took place at the midnight hour in the Upper room.

You cannot be a mover and a shaker when you love sleep. Even the Lord visits His people at night - He showed up to Daniel in a night's vision and He showed up to Solomon in a night's vision. He sends His angels to defend His people at night.

Acts 5:19,
> *But at night an angel of the Lord opened the prison doors and brought them out.*

Same with Peter in Acts 12:7, because the church was praying fervently on his behalf.

In **Exodus 11:4-5**, He vowed to show up at midnight to deal with the generational bondage of his people in Egypt.

> *"Thus says the Lord: 'About midnight I will go out into the midst of Egypt; and all the firstborn in the land of Egypt shall die, from the firstborn of Pharaoh who sits on his throne, even to the firstborn of the female servant who is behind the handmill, and all the firstborn of the animals.*

In **Exodus 12:29**, HE SHOWED UP AND SHOOK EGYPT!

> *..And it came to pass at midnight that the Lord struck all the firstborn in the land of Egypt, from the firstborn of Pharaoh who sat on his throne to the firstborn of the captive who was in the dungeon, and all the firstborn of livestock.*

Have you noticed that your spirit does not sleep at night? It is because spirits do not sleep. God is spirit and He never sleeps nor slumbers. So also angels. The Bible refers to our spirit whenever you see the word *heart* being used. You can see this clearly in **Song of Solomon 5:2**,

> *I sleep, but my heart is awake; It is the voice of my beloved! He knocks, saying, "Open for me, my sister, my love, My dove, my perfect one; For my head is covered with dew, My locks with the drops of the night."*

God is always seeking you out at night. **Psalm 16:7** also talks about His instructions through the spirit in the night watches.

> *I will bless the Lord who has given me counsel; My heart also instructs me in the night seasons.*

The best way to get these instructions to your consciousness is to be awake and in His presence to hear and see many of the instructions. Some of us will just keep sleeping and miss out on this beautiful hour of intimacy. Go and check out all the giants of faith who moved and shook the earth in the Bible or through the ages, they were men and women who prayed through the night watches. I have personally noticed that when I am fasting extensively, my body sleeps less and my spirit man is more awake to hear from the Lord.

PLEASE DO NOT MISTAKE THIS FOR INSOMNIA. Many toss and turn through this crucial moment and wake up grumpy and tired whereas it was the Lord quickening you to pray and download secrets from heaven. The earlier you catch this, the better. When the Lord wakes you to instruct you, after He is done, you sleep back peacefully and wake up refreshed. But if it is the enemy, there will be no peace or rest involved. There are times when you must look into a matter carefully at night to understand the extent of the damage done before the Lord in prayer – you may do it with other prayer warriors or do it alone like **Nehemiah 2:12 and 15**,

> *Then I arose in the night, I and a few men with me; I told no one what my God had put in my heart to do at Jerusalem; nor was there any animal with me, except the one on which I rode. So I went up in the night by the valley, and viewed the wall; then I turned back and entered by the Valley Gate, and so returned.*

Many movers and shakers operated the night watches while fasting and praying in the Bible. As we can see in the case of Esther and Mordecai who went into a three days absolute fast and the Bible records that the same night the king could not sleep in **Esther 6:1**. Your midnight cry can move kings to lose their sleep! I decree that the employer holding down your blessing will lose their sleep until they give you your due promotion in Jesus' name. I declare that all the principalities and powers sitting on your immigration papers will not have any rest until they move your file to the top for approval. As the light of the world, you have been called to shine in darkness. **Matthew 5:14-15,**

> *You are the light of the world. A city that is set on a hill cannot be hidden. Nor do they light a lamp and put it under a basket, but on a lampstand, and it gives light to all who are in the house.*

On the fourth day, God created the greater and lesser lights to rule over the day and the night. Not only will you rise and shine as the greater light during the day but you will begin to rule over the forces of darkness at night as well. From today, you will operate with mastery as a greater light on the earth like our Lord Jesus Christ. You will emerge from this altar as a star to your world! You are already empowered to be a mover and a shaker of the earth just unveil it through your prayer, praise and studying the word of God.

For you to manifest as light, you must be connected to the source of true light through His word.

John 1:1-5 and 9,

> *In the beginning was the Word, and the Word was with God, and the Word was God. He was in the beginning with God. All things were made through Him, and without Him nothing was made that was made. In Him was life, and the life was the light of men. And the light shines in the darkness, and the darkness did not comprehend it. That was the true Light which gives light to every man coming into the world.*

You must live daily in the reality of this word. The truth is that you have no life outside of the word of God, as a believer. So get in the word! Bask in His word! Immerse yourself in the word, soak every ounce you can soak up morning, afternoon and night, believe me, you will emerge as a greater light ruling over the forces of darkness in this age and the age to come. You will be numbered among the movers and shakers of this world!! Amen

It is time to pray!

DAY 4 PRAYER POINTS

1. Thank you Lord for the 4th day of this 21-day journey of transfiguration. Thank you for sending your word in due season.

2. Thank you Lord for the liberty I enjoy in Christ Jesus and for the freedom in my nation to serve you in this land.

3. Thank you Lord for the atoning blood of Jesus that speaks better things than the blood of Abel. Thank You for the remission of sins and blotting out of all evil covenants.

4. Father Lord, empower me as a mover and shaker who prays through the night watches. Instruct my reins through the night and show me secrets about my life, family and nations in Jesus' name.

5. From today, I will take advantage of the midnight watch to commune with You and dismantle the evil altars of my father's house. Like Samson, I am empowered to uproot the gates of resistance obstructing any divine opportunity.

6. As a seed of Abraham through Christ Jesus, I contend with the enemies at the gate and I possess my possessions. I receive the fire to burn the enemy to stubble and the anointing to deliver the oppressed in Jesus' name. Sickness bows to me at the gate. Poverty bows to me at the gate. (Mention anything that needs to bow).

7. As I engage the night watches in prayer and praise, the book of remembrance is opened on my behalf for the payback of all delayed blessings in my marriage, career and ministry. I recover all in Jesus' mighty name!

8. Father Lord, visit my marriage - restore whatever is missing or broken. I address this matter before you Lord

_____ (delay, barrenness, non-achievement etc.) Show the enemy you are my Defender! Let there be nothing missing and nothing broken in Jesus' name.

9. As a light of the world, use me to display your glory. Cause me to shine like never before displaying your splendor and majesty on a daily basis as a mover and shaker of my world. Let my prayer shake the nations in Jesus' name!

10. **COMMUNION:** As I continue on this Mountain of Transfiguration; my spirit becomes fire, my soul receive fire and my body catch the fire of the Holy Ghost like Jesus Christ my Savior. Fire to heal, the anointing to break yokes and the fire to destroy the works of darkness in Jesus' name.

Give thanks for answered prayer.

INSTRUCTION: PRAY OVER YOUR PERSONAL LIST OF REQUEST (**John 16:24**). Observe the midnight watch or 3am watch.

DAY 5
WATCHMAN ARISE!

Today is the fifth day and the number is the number of grace. I pray that like Noah you will find grace in the sight of the Lord. As the word of the Lord declares in **Zechariah 12:8**, may the Lord defend you and your household.

> *"In that day the Lord will defend the inhabitants of Jerusalem; the one who is feeble among them in that day shall be like David, and the house of David shall be like God."*

Verse 10,
> *"And I will pour on the house of David and on the inhabitants of Jerusalem the Spirit of grace and supplication."*

I pray that you will contact the spirit of grace and supplication to intercede for your nation and generation that will result in supernatural transformation!

Today's topic is WATCHMAN ARISE! I want to encourage you as you read this book and pursue the Lord in this fast to take advantage of the early morning watch. In this chapter, we will seek to address some questions and answer them from the pages of scriptures. Questions like: When is the morning watch? Who is a watchman? What does it mean to watch? **Habakkuk 2:1** says,

> *I will stand upon my watch, and set me upon the tower, and will watch to see what he will say unto me, and what I shall answer...*

A watchman is a person who keeps watch in the place of prayer; he prays to God and observes attentively to hear back from the Lord. A watchman is spiritually alert to hear from heaven about any given situation, people or nation.

What is the assignment of a **Watchman**? According to the word of God – a watchman hears from the Lord and warns His people (**Ezekiel 3:17**). A watchman watches unto the Lord and intercedes for God's people according **Isaiah 62:6**,

> *I have set watchmen on your walls, O Jerusalem; They shall never hold their peace day or night. You who make mention of the Lord, do not keep silent.*

From all four Gospels – Matthew, Mark, Luke and John, we see that our Lord Jesus Christ was always watching and praying. It is what marked His supernatural lifestyle on the earth distinctively. He came to show us how to master the flesh and operate in the spirit. He was our perfect example in communicating with the Father and staying in touch with heaven in prayer.

Let's take a look at the Mountain of Transfiguration again,

Luke 9:29-30,

> *As He prayed, the appearance of His face was altered, and His robe became white and glistening. And behold, two men talked with Him, who were Moses and Elijah.*

You will see that while all the others were sleeping, He was communing with heaven.

Verse 32,

> *But Peter and those with him were heavy with sleep; and when they were fully awake, they saw His glory and the two men who stood with Him.*

The Bible records in several places that it was His habit to go and pray alone long before the day breaks;

Mark 1:35,

> *Now in the morning, having risen a long while before daylight, He went out and departed to a solitary place; and there He prayed.*

Like the Lord Jesus Christ, a watchman must be disciplined and spiritually alert; he is someone who guards and protects the heritage of the Lord especially at night. A watchman cannot love sleep and cannot be lazy.

Matthew 26:40-41,

> *Then He came to the disciples and found them sleeping, and said to Peter, "What! Could you not watch with Me one hour? Watch and pray, lest you enter into temptation. The spirit indeed is willing, but the flesh is weak."*

I decree that you will contact the grace of a watchman from the Mountain of Transfiguration in the mighty name of Jesus. Your time of separation in His presence will pay off. You will emerge with power and strength. You will be renewed for Kingdom exploits. The power that you will contact will be just like that of our Lord Jesus Christ, who healed the sick on a regular basis and had demons bow to Him. You will notice that every time He came down from the mountain, the multitude was looking for Him – for example, one of such escapes to the Father's presence was recorded in **Mark 1:32-37, 39:**

> *At evening, when the sun had set, they brought to Him all who were sick and those who were demon-possessed. And the whole city was gathered together at the door. Then He healed many who were sick with various diseases, and cast out many demons; and He did not allow the demons to speak, because they knew Him. Now in the morning, having risen a long while before daylight, He went out and departed to a solitary place; and there He prayed. And Simon and those who were with Him searched for Him. When they found Him, they said to Him, "Everyone is looking for You." And He was preaching in their synagogues throughout all Galilee, and casting out demons.*

He knew where to re-ignite His fire and renew His strength. He did not love sleep like the watchmen described in the book of Isaiah, who loved to slumber. I pray that you will not be like these sloppy watchmen in **Isaiah 56:10,**

> *His watchmen are blind, they are all ignorant; they are all dumb dogs, they cannot bark; Sleeping, lying down, loving to slumber.*

They were supposed to see into the spirit realm but they were blind. They were also very lazy loving to sleep – watchmen are really called to watch when others are snoozing but these ones loved to sleep. They were dumb too. The Lord called the watchman to speak according **Ezekiel 3** and **Ezekiel 33** – they should be speaking with the Lord and speaking with people. As a watchman to this generation, you will not only bark but you will roar like the Lion of the Tribe of Judah! You will be diligent in the place of prayer and will not live a life of compromise. You will not be ignorant but knowledgeable about the things of the Kingdom and you will always know what to do in any given situation by the Spirit of the Lord. As a watchman, when you start getting up very early before dawn, praying and watching for the morning; nothing catches you by surprise. You will know things before they happen just because you are watching for the morning like the Psalmist.

Psalm 130:6,

My soul waits for the Lord more than those who watch for the morning—Yes, more than those who watch for the morning.

You will begin to share God's secret; you will get the first sneak peek on everything He plans to do on the earth just as the word says in

Amos 3:7,

Surely the Lord God does nothing, unless He reveals His secret to His servants the prophets.

When you engage the morning watch – which starts at about 3am in the morning and ends at 6am, you will already know heaven's agenda about each day before the day even begins.

Job 38:12-13,

"Have you commanded the morning since your days began, And caused the dawn to know its place, That it might take hold of the ends of the earth, And the wicked be shaken out of it?"

THE DAWN PATROL

The dawn is a swift and momentous time to take advantage of as a watchman. It is a very brief period just before the morning light. It is a time of utmost importance. As an intercessor, you must be actively engaged in what is called Dawn Patrol: this is the flight mission done very early in the morning to detect the enemy's position and survey the environment in the military — just like the watchman standing on the tower in the times of old. It is still one of the biggest secret of the military today. Many world religions also take advantage of this early morning watch and use it well to control issues. But many Christians get really comfortable at this time and intensify their sleep.

It is very unfortunate that the enemy also takes advantage of this crucial time but thank God Almighty who causes us to triumph in Christ Jesus – He has not only revealed this secret to us but has given us the grace to engage it from today. Help is available to us at this precious hour according to Psalm 46:5,

> *God is in the midst of her, she shall not be moved; God shall help her, just at the break of dawn.*

Please read **Ezekiel 33:1-7**; it essentially explains the duty of a watchman.

> *"Again the word of the Lord came to me, saying, ²"Son of man, speak to the children of your people, and say to them: 'When I bring the sword upon a land, and the people of the land take a man from their territory and make him their watchman, ³when he sees the sword coming upon the land, if he blows the trumpet and warns the people, ⁴then whoever hears the sound of the trumpet and does not take warning, if the sword comes and takes him away, his blood shall be on his own head. ⁵He heard the sound of the trumpet, but did not take warning; his blood shall be upon himself. But he who takes warning will save his life. ⁶But if the watchman sees the sword coming and does not blow the trumpet, and the people are not warned, and the sword comes and takes any person from among them, he is taken away in his iniquity; but his blood I will require at the watchman's hand."*

> *⁷ "So you, son of man: I have made you a watchman for the house of Israel; therefore you shall hear a word from My mouth and warn them for Me.*

This is also a crucial time to address difficult and longstanding issues like Jacob did in **Genesis 32:24, 26**,

> *Then Jacob was left alone; and a Man wrestled with him until the breaking of day. And He said, "Let Me go, for the day breaks." But he said, "I will not let You go unless You bless me!"*

He emerged from that moment a prince with God and prevailed over all the situation that plagued his life and destiny. He got a new name and he had a life transforming encounter that changed his character completely. He became a new man! You also need to travail in the place of prayer to prevail like Jacob, over that seemingly impossible case. You can take up that marital situation before the Lord. You can address those medical reports from the doctors at this moment. You can take over the gates of cities and nations before everyone else is awake.

Jesus spoke to the disciples saying, "*…the spirit is willing but the flesh is weak.*" The flesh cannot watch or pray to God effectively. The Bible says that God is Spirit and those who worship Him must worship in spirit and in truth (**John 4:24**). He is the Baptizer with fire and when He touches you, your prayer life can never be dull again. Ask for the fire of the Lord today! Before now, you may have struggled in the place of prayer but from now on, I am convinced that your prayer altar will catch the fire required for you to set the world ablaze. You will ignite your world and burn to chaff every work of darkness. The entire world will reckon with you because you came to the Mountain of Transfiguration.

It is time to pray!

DAY 5 PRAYER POINTS

1. Thank You Lord for the spirit of grace and supplication. Thank You Lord for the fifth day on this Mountain of Transfiguration. I am grateful for the journey so far.

2. Thank You Lord for the gift of life and family. I am thankful for the breath in me and the Holy Spirit living in me. Thank You Jesus for the baptism of fire!

3. Thank You Lord for the spirit of wisdom and revelation in the knowledge of You; and for calling me as watchman for Your kingdom. Thank You for the Sons of Issachar anointing! 1 Chronicles 12:32.

4. Father Lord, I receive the grace to pray through the morning watch like Jesus so that I can emerge as a wonder to my world. I receive a fresh outpouring of the spirit of grace and supplication so that the smallest in my household will be as David, and the David's like God (Zechariah 12:8&10).

5. From today, I stand upon my watch to hear directly from You, Lord. I enter into the secret place of your pavilion through prayer and praise; I know things before they happen in Jesus' name.

6. Father Lord, I tap into the same anointing as my Lord Jesus Christ to engage the prayer watches and I become a walking solution to the problems that plague humanity on a daily basis in Jesus' name.

7. I am an effective mouthpiece of the gospel and I boldly declare the second-coming of the Lord. I operate with

grace for supernatural exploits - healing the sick and setting captives free in Jesus' name. I attract multitudes for God's glory!

8. From this Mountain of Transfiguration, I emerge a prince as I travail to prevail with God. My name is changed from the old _____ to the new _____. I have a brand new beginning in all areas of my life - newness in my spirit, soul and body in Jesus' name -- from barren to fruitful, single to married, jobless to gainfully-employed, broke to exceedingly blessed, afflicted to anointed.

9. From today, I manifest as spirit, I think as spirit, I walk in the spirit and I pray in the spirit. No more struggling in the flesh as I mount up with the wings of an eagle. I am unstoppable in the place of prayer and intercession in Jesus' name.

10. COMMUNION: Father Lord, quicken my body by the Spirit that raised Jesus from the dead. Make me too hot for the enemy to handle and empower me with the living fire that burns sickness to ashes in Jesus' mighty name.

Give thanks for answered prayer.

INSTRUCTION:

Address one major issue in your life at the morning watch before dawn. Also make a prayer list for your family members and friends that are unsaved. Start praying them into the Kingdom.

DAY 6
RAIN OF FIRE

Today is the sixth day of the fast and the number six represents man because he was created on the sixth day. Man was created for dominion and rulership. He was made in the image and after the likeness of God; so whatever you see in the nature of God will be found in man. God is a RAIN MAKER and He has called many sons to walk as rain makers on the earth. On this sixth day, may you step into your dominion and rulership in Jesus' mighty name! For the past couple of lessons we have been looking at the prayer watches closely – we looked at the midnight watch in Movers and Shakers. We also looked at the early morning watch in Watchman Arise.

In this chapter, we will be looking at the evening watch. The evening watch starts at 3pm and it is also known as the time of the evening sacrifice (see **Daniel 9:21**). I mentioned earlier that when engaging in an extended fast, you may break daily at the time of the evening sacrifice – which is 3pm. I also mentioned that Christ was on the Mountain of Transfiguration with Moses and Elijah for a reason. These prophets of old were only a shadow of what we have in Christ Jesus. Let us take a look at how these two prophets commanded the rain of fire at will and what one of them did at the time of the evening sacrifice.

First of all, Moses was an expert rain maker because of the level of anointing upon him. He could start and stop rain at will. He commanded the rain of fire.

Exodus 9:23-24,

> *Moses stretched out his rod toward heaven; and the Lord sent thunder and hail, and fire darted to the ground. And the Lord rained hail on the land of Egypt. So there was hail, and fire mingled with the hail, so very heavy that there was none like it in all the land of Egypt since it became a nation.*

And he could also stop the rain through his prayers...

Exodus 9:33,

> *So Moses went out of the city from Pharaoh and spread out his hands to the Lord; then the thunder and the hail ceased, and the rain was not poured on the earth.*

When it is about to rain, you will notice heavy clouds. In the Old Testament, thick clouds represent the presence of God. The Lord rides upon the clouds, hail and thunderstorm.

In **Exodus 24:15-18**, Moses went up into the mountain, and a cloud covered the mountain.

> *Now the glory of the Lord rested on Mount Sinai, and the cloud covered it SIX days. And on the seventh day He called to Moses out of the midst of the cloud. The sight of the glory of the Lord was like a consuming fire on the top of the mountain in the eyes of the children of Israel. So Moses went into the midst of the cloud and went up into the mountain. And Moses*

was on the mountain forty days and forty nights.

What set Moses apart from his peers was the fact that he was always walking into the cloud of God's glory. Moses not only commanded physical rain, he also commanded the rain of fire. It was as if God could not have enough of him and he could not have enough of God. He was a man given to much fasting and he lived an exceptional life of unending exploits, He carried divine presence wherever he went.

Like Moses, Elijah was also known to command rain; he was called the prophet of fire.

1 Kings 18:32-35,

Then with these stones he built an altar in the name of the Lord; and he made a trench around the altar large enough to hold two seahs of seed. And he put the wood in order, cut the bull in pieces, and laid it on the wood, and said, "Fill four waterpots with water, and pour it on the burnt sacrifice and on the wood." Then he said, "Do it a second time," and they did it a second time; and he said, "Do it a third time," and they did it a third time. So the water ran all around the altar; and he also filled the trench with water.

Like Elijah you must build an altar of prayer unto the Lord in your life. Is there an altar of the Lord in your home? Do you have a place or time where you meet with the Lord on a daily basis? You must have that secret place, that altar where you meet the Lord perpetually and not haphazardly. Elijah said to the people in verse 21? *"How long will you falter between two opinions? If the Lord is God, follow Him; but if Baal, follow him."* But *the people answered him not a word.* Don't be like the children of Israel who were hot for the Lord one day and cold another day.

Be a son that is mature and display your maturity by gaining mastery in your spiritual walk with the Lord.

During any fast, you must observe at least 3 prayer watches – if you can do more that will be awesome. If you want to get the same result as Elijah; who poured water on the wood three times. You also can adopt this principle of three – you can praise the Lord three times; you can pray three times or search out, study and meditate on the scriptures three times in one day. You may choose to vary the prayer, praise or meditation of the word those three times. Whatever you do, please do not engage in hunger strike, it is a waste of time. Make sure you are not just observing a fast to fulfill a religious obligation or rite; it will not profit you in any way.

After Elijah repaired the altar of the Lord, he laid the woods in order. You must also gather your ammunitions – the weapons or sword of the spirit according to **Ephesians 6:17** and **Hebrews 4:12**. As you go on any fast - produce your cause and bring forth your strong reasons from the word of God. God is only committed to backing His words and not your sentiments or emotions. God answers prayers 100% of the time when we pray according to His will. Not only did he lay the wood in order, he cut the bull in pieces. You will need to sacrifice the flesh on the altar of the Lord. Everything in the flesh has to go! Cut off all the distractions! It has to be cut up in pieces. Ask the Holy Spirit for help you with discipline and self-control. Every sinful tendencies and works of the flesh must go! That stubbornness and unforgiving heart has to be given up on the altar of the Lord.

Then the scriptures concluded that he poured water on the sacrifice 12 times (representing consecration–the washing of the water by the word in **Ephesians 5:26**). **John 17:17** says, *"Sanctify them by your word, your word is truth"*. It was after this consecration that the fire fell.

As we continue reading this chapter in **1 Kings 18**, you will see that he called down the rain of fire in verse 36-39,

> *And it came to pass, at the time of the offering of the evening sacrifice, that Elijah the prophet came near and said, "Lord God of Abraham, Isaac, and Israel, let it be known this day that You are God in Israel and I am Your servant, and that I have done all these things at Your word. Hear me, O Lord, hear me, that this people may know that You are the Lord God, and that You have turned their hearts back to You again." Then the fire of the Lord fell and consumed the burnt sacrifice, and the wood and the stones and the dust, and it licked up the water that was in the trench. Now when all the people saw it, they fell on their faces; and they said, "The Lord, He is God! The Lord, He is God!"*

Like Elijah, if you will seek the Lord earnestly in prayer and in the word during this fast, you will begin to command the rain of fire. The Bible said in **Hosea 10:12**,

> *Sow for yourselves righteousness; Reap in mercy; Break up your fallow ground, For it is time to seek the Lord, Till He comes and rains righteousness on you.*

You can compel a storm in your prayer closet to change the spiritual climate in your family, your city and your nation. Take the time to settle down with God and sow into your own destiny. Nobody will do it for you. You may need to sacrifice many cravings and inordinate affection. If you want to walk in the realm of power, you will need to let go of some T.V shows that compromises your anointing. You must take stock of what you watch, say or do. You must be willing to take a higher walk with the Lord. Then as you fast, you will begin to walk in this order of power to compel the rain of fire.

ASK FOR RAIN

The Bible says to ask!

Zechariah 10:1,

> *Ask the Lord for rain In the time of the latter rain. The Lord will make flashing clouds;He will give them showers of rain,Grass in the field for everyone.*

How do you ask? In prayers…
As we can see Jesus, our perfect example, prayed and compelled the rain of fire wherever He went. He wore this fire as a robe. No wonder His robe was healing the sick without Him touching them because it becomes empowered in prayer and its transformed into lightning.

Luke 9:28-29,

> *Now about eight days after these teachings, Jesus took with Him Peter and John and James and went up on the mountain to pray. And as He was praying, the appearance of His countenance became altered different, and His raiment became dazzling white flashing with the brilliance of lightning.*

John the Baptist proclaimed Him as the one who baptizes with fire in **Luke 3:16**,

> *John answered them all by saying, I baptize you with water; but He Who is mightier than I is coming, the strap of Whose*

sandals I am not fit to unfasten. He will baptize you with the Holy Spirit and with fire.

Your prayer can compel earthquake, thundering and lightning in the spirit realm like the Master!

Revelation 8:3-5,

Then another angel, having a golden censer, came and stood at the altar. He was given much incense, that he should offer it with the prayers of all the saints upon the golden altar which was before the throne. And the smoke of the incense, with the prayers of the saints, ascended before God from the angel's hand. Then the angel took the censer, filled it with fire from the altar, and threw it to the earth. And there were noises, thunderings, lightnings, and an earthquake.

Rain maker arise! You need to take advantage of the evening watch and get into your prayer mode like Elijah. It is about time the rain of fire fell in your city, nation and generation!!

James 5:16b-18,

The effectual, fervent prayer of a righteous man avails much. Elijah was a man with a nature like ours, and he prayed earnestly that it would not rain; and it did not rain on the land for three years and six months. And he prayed again, and the heaven gave rain, and the earth produced its fruit.

PRAISE IS EVEN HIGHER

So if prayer can compel rain, what do you think praise will do? Praise will command a thunderstorm! Get your praises on these 21 days; let the heavens hear your voice and the earth will surely respond to you with increase.

Psalm 67:5-6,

> *Let the peoples praise You, O God; Let all the peoples praise You. Then the earth shall yield her increase; God, our own God, shall bless us.*

The biggest rain of fire came down on the day of Pentecost when about 120 people gathered together praying with one accord – with one passion and one desire – the Lord Jesus!

Acts 2:2-4,

> *And suddenly there came a sound from heaven, as of a rushing mighty wind, and it filled the whole house where they were sitting. Then there appeared to them divided tongues, as of fire, and one sat upon each of them. And they were all filled with the Holy Spirit and began to speak with other tongues, as the Spirit gave them utterance.*

This rain of fire empowers and makes you an incurable witness according to **Acts 1:8,**

> *"But you shall receive power when the Holy Spirit has come upon you; and you shall be witnesses to Me in Jerusalem, and in all Judea and Samaria, and to the end of the earth."*

If you have been touched by this rain of fire, it will show. Just like it did in the lives of the apostles from that day – as we can see that the church of 120 people jumped to 3000 and in the very next chapter miracles, signs and wonders became the order of the day— you will emerge as a wonder to your generation as you seek the Lord in this fast. You will be transfigured to the same image as our Lord and Christ as you fasten your eyes on the mirror of His word.

Let's take a quick look at another example of the prayer watch in **Acts 3:1-10**,

> *Now Peter and John went up together to the temple at the hour of prayer, the ninth hour. (Same as the time of the evening sacrifice) And a certain man lame from his mother's womb was carried, whom they laid daily at the gate of the temple which is called Beautiful, to ask alms from those who entered the temple; who, seeing Peter and John about to go into the temple, asked for alms. And fixing his eyes on him, with John, Peter said, "Look at us." So he gave them his attention, expecting to receive something from them. Then Peter said, "Silver and gold I do not have, but what I do have I give you: In the name of Jesus Christ of Nazareth, rise up and walk." And he took him by the right hand and lifted him up, and immediately his feet and ankle bones received strength. So he, leaping up, stood and walked and entered the temple with them—walking, leaping, and praising God. And all the people saw him walking and praising God. Then they knew that it was he who sat begging alms at the Beautiful Gate of the temple; and they were filled with wonder and amazement at what had happened to him.*

The rain of fire strengthens God's people from weariness to surpassing wonder.

See **Psalm 68:8-9**,

> *The earth shook; The heavens also dropped rain at the presence of God; Sinai itself was moved at the presence of God, the God of Israel. You, O God, sent a plentiful rain, Whereby You confirmed Your inheritance, When it was weary.*

Every weariness of the spirit you have experienced before now, will be burned off by fire on this Mountain of Transfiguration. You are emerging as a changed man! There is a strong connection between God's downpour of the spirit and his people going from strength to strength.

Psalm 84:6-7,
> *As they pass through the Valley of Baca, They make it a spring; The rain also covers it with pools. They go from strength to strength; Each one appears before God in Zion.*

Are you reading this book and you are tired of playing church or exhausted from the curve balls that the enemy has been throwing at you? Are you tired from fighting all the battles on your own or with human strength? Receive the rain of fire today from the BAPTIZER!

You can come to the Baptizer of Fire today. He is waiting for you to ask Him into your heart. He wants to turn your life the right-side up. Are you ready to become a rain-maker like Him, calling down the rain of fire at will? The rain of fire is not something you see with your natural eyes but the effect will be clearly seen by the entire world. Why don't you come and repair that broken altar today and allow Him to consume your flesh with His fire today. When His fire touches your flesh, sickness cannot stand it. Demons cannot survive this fire.

This fire burns up everything messy and filthy, purifying and strengthening the vessel. He wants you to rub minds with him. He called us to dine with Him in **Revelations 3:20**. His table offers the best delicacies that will transform an ordinary mortal to a supernatural being. Draw near to Him now! Get soaked in His power and be ignited by His flame of fire.

It is time to pray!

DAY 6 PRAYER POINTS

1. Thank You Lord for the breaking of another day; Thank You Lord for transforming me daily by your word on this mountain. Thank You for filling me with the knowledge of your will in all wisdom and spiritual understanding.

2. Thank You for the rain of fire and the fresh baptism of power. Thank You Lord for your precious Holy Spirit and for giving me a life-changing encounter with You.

3. Thank You Lord for the blood of Jesus that delivers us from this present evil age and for choosing us in Him before the foundation of the world, that we should be holy and without blame before Him in love.

4. Father Lord, I pray the rain of fire over my prayer altar, my family altar and my church altar in Jesus' name. As I decree a thing, let it be established according to your word. Let my husband, children and entire family contact your fire.

5. My prayer will make bright clouds and my praise will compel thunderstorms in the mighty name of Jesus! Father, let your fire fall over any spiritual or physical drought in my life (Mention the areas of your life that need the rain of fire).

6. I experience divine restoration of all lost time in marriage, career, child-bearing, academics, promotion, opportunities and favor. My finances burst forth at the seams in Jesus' name - I become a financial pillar in the kingdom and a channel of blessing to my generation.

7. Just like Jesus, I will draw the attention of multitudes for salvation and because I operate by a better covenant than Moses and Elijah, I carry the divine presence of the Most High at all times. I pray down a storm and praise down a thunderstorm!

8. My prayer life is no longer a chore and my anointing to praise increases as I saturate the censer in heaven to my father's pleasure. My prayer altar is set on fire as I intercede for my nation and generation in Jesus' name.

9. Just like Jesus, at the sound of my voice demons tremble and sicknesses flee. I draw power from the Holy Spirit to impact my generation for Christ. I contact the fire to storm the kingdom of darkness for the deliverance of the possessed and oppressed in Jesus' name.

10. COMMUNION: From this cup of blessing, I tap into the uncommon strength of Elijah to run my race and from this table I contact the renewing vigor of Moses. I am transformed into the image of my Savior Jesus - I carry fire in my bosom and wear lightning as my robe.

Give thanks for answered prayers.

INSTRUCTION: Take a long standing issue and address it at least 15 minutes through all the PRAYER WATCHES (8 times, in the next 24 hours). Put the wood in order - find two or three scriptures confirming it – The rain of fire will fall.

DAY 7
DAY OF TRUMPETS

Today is seventh day and the number seven connotes completion and perfect rest. **Genesis 2:2-3** says that on the seventh day God ended His work which He had done, and He rested on the seventh day from all His work which He had done, *Then God blessed the seventh day and sanctified it, because in it He rested from all His work which God had created and made.*

YOU WILL ENJOY THE REST OF THE LORD IN ALL AREAS OF YOUR LIFE FROM TODAY IN JESUS' NAME!!

The children of Israel were instructed in **Exodus 20:8-11** to:

> *Remember the Sabbath day, to keep it holy. Six days you shall labor and do all your work, but the seventh day is the Sabbath of the Lord your God. In it you shall do no work: you, nor your son, nor your daughter, nor your male servant, nor your female servant, nor your cattle, nor your stranger who is within your gates. For in six days the Lord made the heavens and the earth, the sea, and all that is in them, and rested the seventh day. Therefore the Lord blessed the Sabbath day and hallowed it.*

The Sabbath represents rest from all labor - I declare that from this seventh day of this fast, you will enter into the rest of the Most High God! No more struggling, no more toiling, no more labor. Your work will become something of joy and fulfillment in the name of Jesus. God worked and enjoyed His work thoroughly; you will not cease enjoying the fruit of your work in Jesus' name. The Sabbath also represents the day of absolute worship to the Lord – a day where you hallow the name of the Lord. A day dedicated to praising and honoring Him. The Sabbath is the seventh day where you honor the Lord in absolute reverence according to His instruction through the pages of scriptures.

We started this journey on the Mountain of Transfiguration exploring how the heavens opened over Jesus and two men communed with him. These two men were Moses and Elijah. I believe that these prophets of old appeared for a reason – we have looked at some of the things they did that made them operate in the supernatural all through their ministry on the earth.

Jesus Himself speaking in **Matthew 5:17** said, *"Do not think that I came to destroy the Law or the Prophets. I did not come to destroy but to fulfill."* Someone might say that these men are from the old dispensation and we are now under a New Covenant – that is very true but **Hebrews 10:1** says that the law, having a shadow of the good things to come. According to **Colossians 2:16-17**, we are no longer being judged by observing new months or Sabbaths like them but our true substance is Christ Jesus. They were a shadow of the real things we enjoy today. They were all written for our example.

1 Corinthians 10:11,
> *Now all these things happened to them as examples, and they were written for our admonition...*

So now, what is the real Sabbath? What does it mean to blow the trumpet or to observe the Sabbath? What does it hold for us as believers? We will see all that in today's lesson DAY OF TRUMPETS.

The Lord called for a fast in **Joel 2:1&15**,
> *Blow the trumpet in Zion, And sound an alarm in My holy mountain! Let all the inhabitants of the land tremble; For the day of the Lord is coming, For it is at hand: Blow the trumpet in Zion, Consecrate a fast, Call a sacred assembly.*

As you continue in this fast, you will need to blow the trumpet of praise in honor and reverence of the King. As you may have noticed from scriptures that the trumpet was the siren that announced that the Lord was about to show up on the earth. When He showed up on Mt. Sinai, the Bible says in Exodus 19, that there was lightning and thundering after the trumpet sounded. The trumpet of praise is always honored by heaven with divine presence.

Exodus 19:16-19,
> *It came to pass... that there were thunderings and lightnings, and a thick cloud on the mountain; and the sound of the trumpet was very loud, so that all the people who were in the camp trembled. And Moses brought the people out of the camp to meet with God.... And when the blast of the trumpet sounded long and became louder and louder, Moses spoke, and God answered him by voice.*

You can compel divine presence through your praise! Did you know that your mouth is your God-given trumpet? **Isaiah 58:1a** says ...*Cry aloud, spare not;Lift up your voice like a trumpet.* **Revelation 1:10** also likened a voice to the sound of a trumpet - *I was in the Spirit on the Lord's Day, and I heard behind me a loud voice, as of a trumpet.*

It was customary for God's people to observe the Sabbath as a perpetual covenant throughout their generations.

See **Exodus 31:12**,

> *And the Lord spoke to Moses, saying, "Speak also to the children of Israel, saying: 'Surely My Sabbaths you shall keep, for it is a sign between Me and you throughout your generations, that you may know that I am the Lord who sanctifies you.*

Verse 14a,

> *You shall keep the Sabbath, therefore, for it is holy to you.*

He repeated the same in **Leviticus 19:30**,

> *'You shall keep My Sabbaths and reverence My sanctuary: I am the Lord...*

He gave specific instructions on how to observe this ordinance in **Leviticus 23:24**,

> *"Speak to the children of Israel, saying: 'In the seventh month, on the first day of the month, you shall have a sabbath-rest, a memorial of blowing of trumpets, a holy convocation.*

It is customary for the Lord's sabbath to be observed with the sound of the trumpet.

Whenever the children of Israel faced a strange battle against their enemy that was the time they sounded the alarm of praise with the trumpet.

See **Numbers 10:9**,

> *"When you go to war in your land against the enemy who oppresses you, then you shall sound an alarm with the trumpets, and you will be remembered before the Lord your God, and you will be saved from your enemies.*

You know why? Because the Lord inhabits the praises of His people. When they sound the alarm of praise, it is to invite the Man of War and the Mighty Man in Battle to the scene. Have you sounded the alarm yet? Have you blown your trumpet in the face of that strange adversity? The forces of darkness cannot stand His praise. They cannot abide in the day of His coming!

The feast of trumpets was an instruction from the Lord for His people to enter every new month with – learn to do the same.

Numbers 10:10,

> *Also in the day of your gladness, in your appointed feasts, and at the beginning of your months, you shall blow the trumpets over your burnt offerings and over the sacrifices of your peace offerings; and they shall be a memorial for you before your God: I am the Lord your God."*

You must not forget that He is the One who brought you thus far! Let's look at two quick example of the day of trumpets in the scriptures. When the children of Israel were shut out of Jericho, He gave the instruction for them to blow the trumpet in **Joshua 6:2-5,**

> *And the Lord said to Joshua: "See! I have given Jericho into your hand, its king, and the mighty men of valor. You shall march around the city, all you men of war; you shall go all around the city once. This you shall do six days. And seven priests shall bear seven trumpets of rams' horns before the ark. But the seventh day you shall march around the city seven times, and the priests shall blow the trumpets. It shall come to pass, when they make a long blast with the ram's horn, and when you hear the sound of the trumpet, that all the people shall shout with a great shout; then the wall of the city will fall down flat. And the people shall go up every man straight before him."*

God's people obeyed and we see the results. Joshua and the people engaged the trumpets at Jericho;

Joshua 6:20,

> *So the people shouted when the priests blew the trumpets. And it happened when the people heard the sound of the trumpet, and the people shouted with a great shout, that the wall fell down flat. Then the people went up into the city, every man straight before him, and they took the city.*

Another example was Jehoshaphat and the people of Judah in a strange battle of trumpets in **2 Chronicles 20:3-4**,

> *And Jehoshaphat feared, and set himself to seek the Lord, and proclaimed a fast throughout all Judah. So Judah gathered together to ask help from the Lord; and from all the cities of Judah they came to seek the Lord.*

2 Chronicles 20:18-19,

And Jehoshaphat bowed his head with his face to the ground, and all Judah and the inhabitants of Jerusalem bowed before the Lord, worshiping the Lord. Then the Levites of the children of the Kohathites and of the children of the Korahites stood up to praise the Lord God of Israel with voices loud and high.

From the scripture above, we see that the people of Judah humbled themselves bowing before the Lord in worship and in a fast. They also rose up very early in the morning...

2 Chronicles 20:20-21,

So they rose early in the morning and went out into the Wilderness of Tekoa; and as they went out, Jehoshaphat stood and said, "Hear me, O Judah and you inhabitants of Jerusalem: Believe in the Lord your God, and you shall be established; believe His prophets, and you shall prosper." And when he had consulted with the people, he appointed those who should sing to the Lord, and who should praise the beauty of holiness, as they went out before the army and were saying: "Praise the Lord, For His mercy endures forever."

You must be willing to take up that case before the Most High God in the early morning watch and praise Him like never before – and I guarantee that YOU WILL HAVE THE SAME RESULTS THEY HAD!!

2 Chronicles 20:22-23,

Now when they began to sing and to praise, the Lord set ambushes against the people of Ammon, Moab, and Mount Seir, who had come against Judah; and they were defeated. For the people of Ammon and Moab stood up against the inhabitants of Mount Seir to utterly kill and destroy them.

And when they had made an end of the inhabitants of Seir, they helped to destroy one another.

It didn't just end there, the reign of Jehoshaphat was marked with rest round about for the rest of his life.

2 Chronicles 20:27-30,
Then they returned, every man of Judah and Jerusalem, with Jehoshaphat in front of them, to go back to Jerusalem with joy, for the Lord had made them rejoice over their enemies. So they came to Jerusalem, with stringed instruments and harps and trumpets, to the house of the Lord. And the fear of God was on all the kingdoms of those countries when they heard that the Lord had fought against the enemies of Israel. Then the realm of Jehoshaphat was quiet, for his God gave him rest all around.

AS YOU PRAISE THE LORD, BLOWING THE TRUMPET OF PRAISE, YOU WILL ENTER INTO YOUR SEASON OF PERFECT REST ROUNDABOUT IN JESUS' NAME.

A final example of the trumpet is at the dedication of the temple during the time of Solomon. We can see the effect of such outpouring of praise in **2 Chronicles 5:13-14,**

Indeed it came to pass, when the trumpeters and singers were as one, to make one sound to be heard in praising and thanking the Lord, and when they lifted up their voice with the trumpets and cymbals and instruments of music, and praised the Lord, saying: "For He is good, For His mercy endures forever," that the house, the house of the Lord, was filled with a cloud, so that the priests could not continue ministering because of the cloud; for the glory of the Lord filled the house of God.

God's glory cloud filled the house just like the cloud descended on the Mountain of Transfiguration with Jesus. You need to get into the habit of uncommon praise. You can bring down the glory clouds through your mouth trumpet. You can place a demand on the blood covenant you have with Lord through His Son Jesus Christ. It makes the Him respond to your earthly trumpet with His heavenly trumpet.

And we all know that when He blows His trumpet His entourage shows up. If you desire to walk in the realm of consistent victory, then you must adopt a lifestyle of praise and worship. Let your distinct trumpet be heard on a regular basis in heaven and believe me, the earth will reverberate with the downpour of the trumpet from heaven.

It is time to pray!

DAY 7 PRAYER POINTS

1. Thank You Lord for the seventh day in this uncommon journey; I'm thankful for double perfection. Thank You for the rest that remains for the people of God!

2. Thank You Lord for your sustaining grace on this Mountain of Transfiguration. Thank You for winning all the strange battles and equipping me for the journey ahead.

3. Thank You Lord for the Feast of Trumpets where you have covenanted to defeat all my enemies by the blood of everlasting covenant.

4. Thank You Lord for teaching me the secret weapon of praise and worship. Thank You Lord for showing up with

your trumpet; fighting all my visible and invisible battles as I blow my trumpet of praise.

5. Thank You Lord for showing me the perfection in praise and for blessing me with rest round-about in all the areas of my life – my marriage, my academics, my finances, my children, my health, my ministry and the work of my hands.

6. As I engage the Feast of Trumpets, let Your glory cloud descend upon my life. Let me hear Your instructions clearly for the next level and grant me unusual intel for the strange battles in my life or family in Jesus' name.

7. Father Lord, perfect that which concerns me today. Perfect that which concerns me this seventh day. Perfect that which concerns me this year with double perfection; let all that you have in stock for my divine destiny be released by vision and revelation in Jesus' name.

8. Lord, let the anointing of rest speak for me in every area of my life and calling. I speak rest to my home, rest to my job, rest in my academics, rest in my ministry, rest when I wake up and rest when I lie down to sleep. I enter into a covenant of rest through praise!

9. As I engage the mystery of the Day of Trumpet at the prayer watches, let yokes be broken, let the fetters of iron be destroyed. I decree that every wall of resistance is broken down and the prison doors of affliction be shattered into pieces in Jesus' mighty name. Let your heavenly trumpet sound over every area of my life.

10. COMMUNION: On this Day of the Trumpet, I praise my way into unlimited breakthrough and I declare permanent

victory over _____ (barrenness, stagnation, household wickedness, failure at the edge of breakthrough, poverty, shame, sickness, ungodly delay, night terrors, strange battles, misfortune and evil family trends) in Jesus' name.

Give thanks for answered prayers

INSTRUCTION: Take all the matters that need to be addressed before the Lord at the midnight watch - BLOW THE TRUMPET - Don't ask for anything but praise Him for every single one of them.

DAY 8
NEW DAY NEW NAME

Today is the eighth day and the number eight represent a new beginning. On this Mountain of Transfiguration you will emerge with a new name and a new beginning from today in Jesus' name. You will move from the bottom to the top and from zero to hero. You will experience a brand new beginning with your entire household and you will also become an embodiment of wonder to your world. When Christ stepped down from the Mountain of Transfiguration, He was a walking wonder. He healed the sick and set the captives free. As you continue on this journey, demons will begin to tremble before you like Christ Jesus. He came down with His face glistening with light, I declare that you will shine and your glory will be seen by all those who mocked at you before now. You will noise the fame of the Lord abroad as you become a Transformer in His hands in Jesus' name. AMEN!

While the whole world is sleeping and you are observing the prayer watches, you will begin to change from inside out and the glory of the Lord will transform the old you into a new man just like it happened with our Master Jesus (Luke 9:29). Jesus began to pray and the disciples tried to stay awake, but their eyes grew heavier and heavier and finally they all fell asleep. When they awakened, they looked over at Jesus and saw something inexplicable happening. Jesus was changing before their eyes, beginning with His face. It seemed to glow. The glow spread, and even His clothing took on a blinding whiteness. Then, two figures appeared in the glorious radiance emanating from Jesus...

Can you imagine the stigma or label this family had to carry for so long? The boy had special needs as would be the correct terminology used in psychology today. His father had to carry him everywhere and pay close attention to him. For someone like that, he will have almost no other life but to care for this only child. Everything revolves around this special need. The mother was not even mentioned, peradventure she was gone or even dead. Who knows? The fact remains that the boy was seriously oppressed and possessed by a spirit of convulsion and epilepsy. He was possibly retarded in functioning and the father said it was 24/7. That means the father hardly knew the true personality of his son - the demon had completely taken over.

From this passage of scripture, we can see that this was a very shameful and painful situation for not only the boy but his entire family. The demon was a very violent one - a spirit of insanity. I am sure the father's livelihood would have been impacted because he must ensure that the boy had childcare if he had to go to work and earn any living to support his family. It was also obvious that few people will want to watch this boy for an extended period of time. To top it all, he lamented that he was his only child! That shows there was a form of barrenness in that particular family, else why will there be no other children? There is no telling that before Christ touched this boy, he had a future of getting married or having his own children. That meant that the family tree would have become bare and completely fruitless – stampeded by the forces of darkness. Who knows if that was a generational problem that ran in their family?

What a complicated case! The future was bleak for the father and son before Christ showed up. There was no marital bliss for the father or marital future for the son. There was no rest for that family, the demon tortured both of them day and night. Their joy must have been stolen, their dignity shattered. Their finances must have been impacted greatly and if the father had a job - he must have been known at work as the man who called in all the time because of his family emergencies. What a life! I am sure that they would have had very few friends, if any at all because the boy was known to scream violently – it was not a pretty sight and no one would really want to associate with these ones on a daily basis. That was their story before Christ stepped down from the Mountain of Transfiguration.

When Jesus showed up with the power that silences demons and shatters the chains of wickedness, their story changed. The father and son got a new beginning and a new name. It was a new day for both of them. The father's name changed from the father of a lunatic to the father of the healed. His sorrow became joy, his tears turned to unlimited laughter, and he came out from seclusion to the open ground of wonder and amazement. The stigma became an enigma; he was no longer stigmatized. That singular encounter changed their lives forever. Now the boy could be who God called him to be in his right frame of mind; he could do what his mates were doing in school or chosen career. He could decide to get married and have his own children if he so chooses.

Barrenness was cured and his marital destiny addressed. From this mountain, as you pray like Christ prayed, you will have two results. Not only will you experience a brand new beginning having a new name, but you will also be empowered as the one setting the captives free. Like Jesus, when you show up, solutions show up. Wherever you appear from today, deliverance will become the order of the day. You will be an Eternal Excellency, a joy unto many generations. Because as Jesus is, so are we in this world.

I declare that if you are unmarried, you will become happily married in Jesus' mighty name.

Isaiah 62:2 & 4,
> *You shall be called by a new name, Which the mouth of the Lord will name. You shall no longer be termed Forsaken, Nor shall your land any more be termed Desolate; But you shall be called Hephzibah, and your land Beulah; For the Lord delights in you, And your land shall be married.*

If you have been called barren before now, your name is changing on this Mountain of Transfiguration to the father or mother of many nations - kings and princes will come out of you. I speak life to that womb right now! I address that spirit of infertility that will not allow you to conceive or maintain a pregnancy or carry the baby to term in the name of Jesus, I cast it out and make the evil habitations desolate by fire! No more miscarriage! No more abortion of life and destiny in Jesus' mighty name!

If you were struggling with the work of your hands before today, receive a new beginning. You will no longer struggle nor toil any more. You will not experience shame any longer; that affliction that makes you shed the secret tears of sorrow will become a thing of open magnificence and wonder reflecting the glory of our God and King. Just like this father and son, your story will change.

In case there is anyone reading this book and the doctors have given you an evil report or told you that there is nothing they can do about your medical situation. Jesus has the final say! He is the Great Physician and He can make impossibilities possible. He can reverse the irreversible. That chronic condition is terminated today in the Name above every other name. Receive deliverance from that strange affliction and become empowered by the Holy Spirit not only to be healed but to deliver others that are sick in Jesus' name. By virtue of the New Covenant in Christ Jesus, you have the power to replicate all that Christ did while he walked on this side of eternity and more. He said in **John 14:12-14**,

> *"Most assuredly, I say to you, he who believes in Me, the works that I do he will do also; and greater works than these he will do, because I go to My Father. And whatever you ask in My name, that I will do, that the Father may be glorified in the Son. If you ask anything in My name, I will do it."*

But Christ did not do it by mouthing the words with nonchalance or confessing victory casually. He took the time to pray and paid the price of fasting on a regular basis to silence the flesh. He was Spirit and He was also flesh just like you and I. As a born again Christian, you have the same spirit that dwelt in Christ. You were bestowed with that same spirit at New Birth. Jesus was always in touch with the Father to see what the next agenda of heaven was – you know heaven's agenda for your generation. Receive the anointing to know things before they happen. Receive the grace to be in constant touch with the Father.

If you want to walk like Christ walked, then you must pray like He prayed. He died and bestowed the grace to live a victorious life of exploits, do not make His grace of non-effect.

The secret of Jesus' earthly ministry was His constant communion with the Father. He raised the dead and destroyed demonic yokes by intensifying His anointing in the place of prayer and fasting. See another example in **John 11:1**,

> *"Now a certain man was sick, Lazarus of Bethany, the town of Mary and her sister Martha."*

Verse 6,
> *"So, when He heard that he was sick, He stayed two more days in the place where He was."*

My question is: What was he doing for two more days? I strongly believe that He was praying and we can see that He referred to this prayer at the tomb of Lazarus in **John 11:41-44**:

> *Then they took away the stone from the place where the dead man was lying. And Jesus lifted up His eyes and said, "Father, I thank You that You have heard Me. And I know that You always hear Me, but because of the people who are standing by I said this, that they may believe that You sent Me." Now when He had said these things, He cried with a loud voice, "Lazarus, come forth!" And he who had died came out bound hand and foot with grave clothes, and his face was wrapped with a cloth. Jesus said to them, "Loose him, and let him go."*

Notice that verse 41 said where the dead man was laying. Lazarus had lost his name, his life and calling. He had no identity anymore but was simply referred to as the dead man. Even his sister did not use his name anymore but when Jesus showed up, He called him by name, "LAZARUS, come forth!"

He got a brand new beginning and we know the rest of the story. You may have lost your identity with the last crisis you faced; maybe you even wear the pain of the last battle like a badge. It is time to drop that coat of arm for the breastplate of righteousness. It is time to walk out on depression, fear and low self-esteem.

IT IS TIME TO WALK OUT OF THE TOMB OF FAILURE AND MEDIOCRITY!!

It is time to walk into the full dominion God has called us to. Lazarus became more famous after he came back to life than before he died. I am sure that he would have become an eligible bachelor after his testimony spread through the land. I wonder what disease killed him; he was now free from that sickness when Christ called him out. He must have conquered that familial trend of marital delay or failure – if you read properly, you will notice that none of the sisters were also married at the time.

I also mentioned a man earlier who travailed to prevail in **Genesis 32:24, 28**:

> *Then Jacob was left alone; and a Man wrestled with him until the breaking of day. And He said, "Your name shall no longer be called Jacob, but Israel; for you have struggled with God and with men, and have prevailed."*

He came out with a new name! A supplanter transformed into a prince with God. What is that name you want to leave behind? What is that shameful past that has plagued you thus far? You can take on a new name today. You can walk out on that demonic affliction and silence the demons forever if you will just walk into the inner recesses of the Lord's presence.

You can command a legion and they will obey you. He gave you the power to tread upon ancient serpents and scorpions already, according to **Luke 10:19**.

It is time to pray!

DAY 8 PRAYER POINTS

1. Thank You Lord for calling me out of the congregation of the dead into a lively hope. Thank You for translating me from the kingdom of darkness to the kingdom of light.

2. Thank You Lord for empowering me on this 21 days journey; I am grateful for strengthening me by your Spirit in my inner man to fast, praise and observe the prayer watches.

3. Thank You Lord for the gift of life and for my family, friends and loved ones. I am grateful for my teachers and mentors - for those who labor over me in word and prayer.

4. Father Lord, on this eighth day, grant me a brand new beginning. Give me a new name; move me from the bottom to the top and take me from zero to hero in Jesus' name. Change my name from _____ to _____. FILL IN THE BLANK. *E.g. Loser-winner, failure-success, barren-fruitful, tail-head, zero-hero, sick-healed, weak-strong, single-married, sorrowful-joyful, stagnated-elevated, jobless-employer*

5. From today, anoint me as a walking wonder to my world. Let your miracles, signs and wonder be my identity from this mountain of transfiguration. Set me on fire to set the captives free!

6. I receive the anointing to pray when others are tired and the grace to fast when others are feasting. I activate the power within me to tread upon ancient serpents and scorpions in Jesus' mighty name.

7. Father Lord, terminate every stigma in my family-line and destroy every generational yoke by the anointing of fire. I refuse to carry any stigma of shame in my marriage, career or ministry - my children cannot be troubled because they bear the marks of Christ Jesus.

8. Lord, make me a mountain dweller like Jesus. Open my eyes to see your glory and open my ears to hear your voice. Grant me insight to heaven's agenda per time; let me move with the glory cloud in Jesus' name.

9. I join my faith with all those praying on this mountain of transfiguration that all evil medical reports are nullified in Jesus' name. All the strange diseases and demonic afflictions are shattered by fire. We agree according to **Matthew 18:18-20** that we do greater works from today.

Matthew 18:18-20, *"Assuredly, I say to you, whatever you bind on earth will be bound in heaven, and whatever you loose on earth will be loosed in heaven. "Again I say to you that if two of you agree on earth concerning anything that they ask, it will be done for them by My Father in heaven. For where two or three are gathered together in My name, I am there in the midst of them."*

10. COMMUNION: By this blood of Jesus and His flesh transform me by fire. Let me become an expert at solving complicated problems. I am healed and I carry healing virtue, I am wise and teach others wisdom, I am free and set others free and I am blessed to be a blessing to my generation!

Give thanks for answered prayers.

INSTRUCTION: Write down all the old names that brought shame before today and go to the Lord alone at the midnight watch to get a new name(s). He will turn that shame for His fame!

DAY 9

POWER TO CONCEIVE

Today is the ninth day of the fast and the number nine represents fruitfulness. It takes about nine months for a pregnant woman to carry a baby to full term. The Bible refers to this as the time of life –I decree that from today, you will take delivery of all that heaven has ordained for you in life and destiny in Jesus name!

Hebrews 11:11,

> *By faith Sarah herself also received power to conceive a child, when she was long past the age for it, because she considered God Who had given her the promise to be reliable and trustworthy and true to His word.*

I declare that anyone called barren like Sarah will receive the power to conceive and the strength to deliver in Jesus' mighty name. We will attempt to address both spiritual barrenness and physical barrenness in today's lesson.

When Jesus came down from the Mountain of Transfiguration in **Luke 9:37-41,** we see that a man cried out to Him about his demon possessed son. He also lamented that he was his only child! Before that day, no one could help him.

The doctors could not help him, the Pharisees could not help him and even the disciples of Jesus could not help him. Like I mentioned earlier; his whole life must have been put on hold to take care of his son. It is clear that there was a form of barrenness in this family because he had no other children? He said he was his only child. I have seen many people who experience barrenness after having one child. It can be due to many reasons that time will not permit us to address here but I know without a doubt that God can visit any womb under the yoke of barrenness.

I have personally experienced the hand of the Lord in this area. After our second child, we decided to wait for a couple of years before having any other children but the couple of years turned into several years of waiting but today, we have a precious testimony from the Lord after the long wait. Not only did we get a very healthy baby, but the specific gender that we asked from the Lord and many other specific details about the child. It was also the best pregnancy I ever had, the entire nine month was full of supernatural energy and the unusual zeal of the Lord was available for me to pray. If you have ever been pregnant before, I am sure you can appreciate the need for constant grace and strength to pray. He upheld me throughout in perfect health and strength such that the doctors used to joke that I was too boring. Praise God for boring medical cases in the life of His children.

Back to the foot of the mountain, we can see that not only was the father who cried out to Jesus barren after having this boy, but the boy himself had a barren future because of the seizures and torment he suffered. Without the deliverance he encountered that day when the Master showed up, I doubt he would have grown up to marry, not to talk of having children of his own. So that means the family tree was barren and totally fruitless - stunted by the forces of darkness.

Who knows if that was a generational problem that ran through their family tree? Whether it was from his father's house or his mother side of the family was completely irrelevant. When Jesus stepped into their situation, not only did the father and son get a new beginning on that day, the barrenness in their lives was terminated forever. Their story changed instantly and they became the talk of the entire town. What fruit is missing in your life? In what area are you experiencing barrenness? Are you physically seeking the fruit of the womb or are you spiritually barren? Are you broke and begging all the time? Are you always experiencing set back such that you have become an expert playing catch-up with your peers? I don't know what label you have been given in the past. Even if you have been called barren before now, your name is changing on this Mountain of Transfiguration! You will no longer be called barren! Your name is FRUITFUL!!

Do not be afraid because the Lord said in Genesis 17:6, *I will make you exceedingly fruitful; and I will make nations of you, and kings shall come from you.* From today, your name is now called the father of nations and the joyful mother of many generations - kings and princes will come out of you. You are exceedingly fruitful! I speak life to that womb right now! I address that spirit of barrenness and miscarriage, miscarriage of children and the abortion of destiny. I cast you out and make your habitation desolate! Be burnt to chaff by the fire of the Holy Ghost. I declare today is the end of that affliction that will not allow you to conceive or carry your baby to term in the mighty name of Jesus!

Did you also know that the enemy is always attacking the godly seed? Has it ever occurred to you that you may be experiencing that delay because of the greatness you carry inside? If you look through scriptures, you will see that when a great destiny is about to be born - there is usually an ungodly delay or an unusual attack against the seed. Like in the time of Moses when the ruling principality issued a death sentence for all male born children. Why? Because the deliverer of Israel from the generational bondage of slavery of over 400 years was about to be born. A similar thing happened when our Lord Jesus Christ was born. The forces of darkness issued a death sentence for all little children under the age of three just because the enemy heard that a great STAR has been born. The greater the destiny, the greater the attack. If your star has been monitored before now, like Elijah the prophet of fire declared, let the fire of God fall and devour every evil monitor in Jesus name. That godly vision must be birthed and mature to fruition. I declare that the godly seed in your life will be brought to life in Jesus' mighty name.

As an expectant parent, looking up to God for the fruit of the womb, you need to settle down with the Lord during this 21 days fast and ask for the specific instruction concerning that special child you were called to bear - most of the time, the children with special assignments come out of the womb of delay. Examples are Isaac, Jacob, Joseph - you can see that barrenness ran in that family. Abraham and Sarah experienced it, Isaac and Rebekah experienced it and so also did Jacob and Rachel. Possibly because the enemy was threatened by them or because the Lord would not release the special destinies without first gaining the attention of their parents. Samson was a special child with a unique assignment; his parents experienced delay but gave birth to him after they got the specific instruction on how to raise him. He was a great judge of Israel for about 40 years.

Zechariah and Elizabeth also experienced delay in having children because they had a purpose to fulfill by bringing forth the forerunner of our Lord Jesus Christ - John the Baptist. The timing of his birth was relevant and it was crucial for it to coincide with the timing of the birth of Jesus Christ. If you can understand heaven's agenda concerning your unborn child, you will stop running helter-skelter. You will stop running from pillar to post - it is God who makes and gives children according to **Ecclesiastes 11:5**,

> *As you do not know what is the way of the wind, Or how the bones grow in the womb of her who is with child, So you do not know the works of God who makes everything.*

SETTLE DOWN WITH HIM! He knows about every single conception before it happened - **Jeremiah 1:5** says *before I formed you I knew you...* He intricately wove each one of us together from our mother's womb.

We know the story of a woman who was barren for many years in the Bible - one day, she settled down with the Lord and made a vow at the time when the entire land was corrupt and there was no true prophet who feared the Lord. She made a vow saying if the Lord will give her a son, she will give him back to God as a prophet in **1 Samuel 1:10-11** ....*she prayed to the Lord and wept in anguish. Then she made a vow and said, "O Lord of hosts, if You will indeed look on the affliction of Your maidservant and remember me, and not forget Your maidservant, but will give Your maidservant a male child, then I will give him to the Lord all the days of his life, and no razor shall come upon his head."* She got the key to unlock her womb forever! God honored her vow and not only did she have Samuel, she had five more children according to **1 Samuel 2:21**, *And the Lord visited Hannah, so that she conceived and bore three sons and two daughters. Meanwhile the child Samuel grew before the Lord.*

In order to reverse that yoke of barrenness, you need to go back to the Author and Completer of destinies! Ask Him for the specific instructions about that seed you carry on your inside. You have been destined to birth greatness. Receive the power to conceive and the strength to deliver in Jesus' name. As for that individual experiencing barrenness in your spiritual life and destiny, you have attempted to work it out thus far with human strength. The Bible says *by strength shall no man prevail* - go back to the One who made you. Ask Him for the specifics of your journey. Jabez did, Jacob did and they both got new names after they touched heaven with their heartfelt prayer; their fruitless efforts became fruitful increase. Honor replaced shame. Affluence replaced poverty. As you seek the Lord on this Mountain of Transfiguration, I declare that you will be transformed into the true image and likeness of your Maker. Your destiny is delivered from the yoke of barrenness and profitless hard labor. You will no longer be termed forsaken. You will always know the way forward. You will be intimated about the details of your life and assignment. You will not be stranded in life anymore in Jesus' mighty name.

We can see from the Word of God that when God is talking about fruitfulness, He addresses both physical and spiritual fruitfulness.

Deuteronomy 7:13-14,

And He will love you and bless you and multiply you; He will also bless the fruit of your womb and the fruit of your land, your grain and your new wine and your oil, the increase of your cattle and the offspring of your flock, in the land of which He swore to your fathers to give you. You shall be blessed above all peoples; there shall not be a male or female barren among you or among your livestock.

According to the word of the Lord, you shall not be barren in Jesus' name! God is concerned about your total and complete fruitfulness in all spheres of your existence according to **Deuteronomy 28:4**,

"Blessed shall be the fruit of your body, the produce of your ground and the increase of your herds, the increase of your cattle and the offspring of your flocks.

RECEIVE THE SPIRIT OF FRUITFULNESS TODAY IN JESUS' NAME.

The two men on the Mountain of Transfiguration experienced supernatural provision and multiplication – Elijah ate angel's food (**1 Kings 19:5-8**); Moses ate angel's food (**Psalm 78:24,25**) and Jesus our Lord ate angel's food when he had finished fasting for 40 days and 40 nights in **Matthew 4:11** and **Mark 1:13**. These two men not only ate from heaven's table, but fed others by divine provision. Moses fed millions in the wilderness with manna and quail, Elijah's anointing sustained a widow's family for 3 and half years and our perfect example, Christ, was daily walking in abundance and multiplying provision feeding the multitudes. He walked in the miraculous without struggle. He carried multiplication with Him wherever He went. It takes a son to manifest the nature of his father. Are you a child of God or the son of the Most High? Multiplication is in your DNA already. All you need to do is to bring it out or stir it up like Paul told Timothy, in the place of prayer. You are His ambassador. He lives in you, as He is, so are you in this world. Go and do likewise! You are a channel of blessing to this generation.

It is time to pray!

DAY 9 PRAYER POINTS

1. Thank You Lord for the boldness to approach Your throne of grace and the ability to obtain mercy and find grace in the time of need. Thank You for the blood of Jesus!

2. Thank You Lord for the vibrant breath of life in me today. Thank You for sparing my life and bringing to nought every counsel of the enemy concerning me.

3. Thank You for the 21 days Mountain of Transfiguration - changing me, transforming me, strengthening me. Thank You for the eye-opening encounters from the first day.

4. Father Lord, I receive the power to conceive and the strength to carry to term my godly seed in Jesus' name. I destroy every yoke of miscarriage and break every spirit of abortion of life or destiny by the blood of Jesus. I am exceedingly fruitful!

5. Father Lord, visit me on this Mountain of Transfiguration like You visited Sarah. Do to me as you have spoken. Let me enter a season of unending laughter; let everyone laughing at me begin to laugh with me in Jesus' name.

6. Lord, baptize me afresh with the anointing of multiplication. I declare according to Your word that the fruit of my body, (my children), my strength, my health are blessed! The produce of my land - my provision, my work, my dwelling and real estate are blessed beyond measure in Jesus' name.

7. Lord, I receive strength to conceive and bear children that are beautiful inside out like Moses, passionate for the Lord like Samuel and consumed by His zeal like Jesus. My children will

wax strong in the spirit, grow in wisdom and favor in Jesus' name.

8. Father, show me the assignment for which You separated me from my mother's womb; reveal to me the purpose for which You ordained me. Bring to pass every detail in Your books according to the days fashioned for me in Jesus' name (Say this prayer for each of your children too).

9. FOR THOSE EXPECTING OR WAITING: My pregnancy will not suffer miscarriage or medical error. Neither will I bring forth children for trouble - no medical complication. I will have my children naturally and will enjoy supernatural delivery like the Hebrew women because I operate under a better covenant in Christ Jesus. (Intercede for someone if your quiver is full).

10. COMMUNION: On this mountain, let great destinies that have been delayed be delivered with speed. See to it that everyone comes back next year with their testimonies like You said to Sarah in **Genesis 18:14**.

Give thanks for answered prayers

INSTRUCTION:

(1) As an expectant parent, ask the Lord for the name of the child God wants you to raise for Him with the specific assignment (e.g. Jesus and John).

(2) If you are experiencing barrenness in your journey, ask the Lord for a new name and the specific details of your assignment.

DAY 10

LION NOT A DOG

This is the tenth day and **Zechariah 8:23** says, *"Thus says the Lord of hosts: 'In those days ten men from every language of the nations shall grasp the sleeve of a Jewish man, saying, "Let us go with you, for we have heard that God is with you."'"* From this mountain, men will begin to follow you to the Lord's house as they see the impact of transfiguration on your life. You will emerge from this mountain a completely transformed individual. You will move from the natural realm of things to supernatural exploits like our Master Jesus. He walked on this earth confronting the works of darkness and He is seated on the throne now as the Lion of the tribe of Judah; the Root of David - who has prevailed! He is a Lion and so are you.

Jesus is the LION OF THE TRIBE OF JUDAH; He did not turn back from the lions of this world. He confronted them and defeated them completely. He disarmed them and broke their teeth! So why do many Christians tremble before demons and turn away with a defeatist mentality? The settling mantra is from Ecclesiastes 9:4, *But for him who is joined to all the living there is hope, for a living dog is better than a dead lion.* Let me announce to you: You are not a dead lion neither are you a living dog! You are a living and empowered lion, made after the image and likeness of God. This scripture does not apply to you. You are no longer operating under the old covenant neither are you trapped under the Adamic dispensation; where the law of sin and condemnation ruled - you have been called out by the Lion of Judah who has prevailed! You are a supernatural lion!

WHAT IS A LION KNOWN FOR?

The lion is bold! The Bible says in **Proverbs 28:1**, *The wicked flee when no one pursues, But the righteous are bold as a lion* and Proverbs 30:30 says, *A lion, which is mighty among beasts - does not turn away from any.* If you look through the scriptures you can see that Jesus made an open show of the fake lions of this world. God roars as a lion and so does His prophet according to **Amos 3:7-8**,

> *Surely the Lord God does nothing, Unless He reveals His secret to His servants the prophets. A lion has roared! Who will not fear? The Lord God has spoken! Who can but prophesy?*

The lion is also very selective of the company it keeps - lions usually hunt together with other lions and raise their family in packs. They don't roll with dogs or hyena. It is ironical that the man called Judah himself made terrible mistakes because of the wrong company he kept - he hung unto the wrong friends and married into a wrong family in **Genesis 39**, but thanks be to God who knows how to turn a story for His glory. Today, our Lord Jesus Christ came from that specific line of Judah. He turned the dysfunctional mess in the line of Judah into a dynamic message in the first chapter in the book of Matthew.

WHAT IS THE DIFFERENCE BETWEEN LION AND DOGS?

Dogs eat crap. **Proverbs 26:11** says, *As a dog returns to his own vomit, So a fool repeats his folly.* Prayerless watchmen are also described as dogs in **Isaiah 56:10-11**,

> *His watchmen are blind, They are all ignorant; They are all dumb dogs, They cannot bark; Sleeping, lying down, loving to slumber. Yes, they are greedy dogs Which never have enough. And they are shepherds who cannot understand; They all look to their own way, Every one for his own gain, from his own territory. And when the atmosphere is really scary, a dog is known to cower in fear.*

Ecclesiastes 9:4 does not apply to you – you have been set free from that ignorance from today! You are no longer in captivity but you have been empowered to set others free. **Hosea 4:6** says ignorance destroys and so does **Isaiah 5:13**,

> *Therefore my people have gone into captivity, Because they have no knowledge; Their honorable men are famished, And their multitude dried up with thirst. But through knowledge will the righteous be delivered!*

I would also like to mention at this point that the enemy is also referred to in scriptures "as a lion" or "like a roaring lion seeking whom he may devour"...he is not real but a cheap copy. There are lions and there are lions! The lions of this world are only a cheap copy of the original. David described the forces of darkness as a raging lion and dogs in **Psalm 22:13, 16, 21**:

> *They gape at Me with their mouths, Like a raging and roaring lion. For dogs have surrounded Me; The congregation of the wicked has enclosed Me. Save Me from the lion's mouth?*

He prayed against these lions of wickedness in **Psalm 35:17**,

Lord, how long will You look on? Rescue me from their destructions, My precious life from the lions.

Praise the Lord for divine insight! Moses wrote in **Psalm 91:13**,

You shall tread upon the lion and the cobra, The young lion and the serpent you shall trample underfoot.

And the patriarchs of old had the testimony in **Hebrews 11:33** that through faith they subdued kingdoms, worked righteousness, obtained promises, stopped the mouths of lions. Daniel was a typical example of one who stopped the mouth of lions in **Daniel 6** - please read this passage in your own spare time. He was a supernatural lion, so the regular lions could not eat him. How did he manifest his lion nature? Through prayer!

In our main text for this fast, we can see Jesus rebuking the demon (fake lions) with boldness (**Luke 9:37-42**). What had Jesus been doing on the mountain? Fasting and praying. His divine nature manifested every time He engaged this divine secret. We are just like Him and we are able to manifest our true nature as we spend time looking at the mirror of His word during this fast (**2 Corinthians 3:18**).

The spirit also transforms us daily, so key into the spirit and pray like your life depends on it. My prayer is that you will eat the food of true lions as you abide in the spirit on this Mountain of Transfiguration. Lions eat fresh meat and drink honey. The word of God has been described as both meat and honey. You have the Lion of Judah dwelling on your inside, It is time to express your divine nature as a lion - the size of a lion is known by the size of his roar. You must mature in the spirit. You have to move from consuming milk as a baby to eating STRONG MEAT. It will also interest you to know that baby lions have to depend on mature lions to feed and sometimes they starve to death. Please grow up! You cannot afford to be a baby lion anymore (**Psalm 34:10**). You are a lion king!

Note that strong meat belongs to sons... **Hebrews 5:12-14,**

> *For though by this time you ought to be teachers, you need someone to teach you again the first principles of the oracles of God; and you have come to need milk and not solid food. For everyone who partakes only of milk is unskilled in the word of righteousness, for he is a babe. But solid food belongs to those who are of full age, that is, those who by reason of use have their senses exercised to discern both good and evil.*

Get the word anyhow! The mature lion is a ferocious hunter and he will skillfully get what he wants when he is hungry. The lion is known to be very active at night and is known to hunt especially at dawn. Engage the midnight watch and early morning watch before the dawn breaks. Don't sleep through the challenges and problems like the dumb dogs described in **Isaiah 56:10-11**. Be hungry for the Lord – unleash the lion within through prayer especially praying in the spirit (**Romans 8:26-27**).

Jude 1:20,
> *Building up yourself in the most holy faith praying in the Holy Ghost*

Speaking and praying in tongues allows you to rub minds with God the Holy Spirit and download divine secrets. The Teacher will offer you unusual intel in spiritual warfare.

1 Corinthians 2:6-7, 9-16,
> *But as it is written:"Eye has not seen, nor ear heard, Nor have entered into the heart of man The things which God has prepared for those who love Him." But God has revealed them to us through His Spirit. For the Spirit searches all things, yes, the deep things of God. For what man knows the things of a man except the spirit of the man which is in him? Even so no one knows the things of God except the Spirit of God. Now we have received, not the spirit of the world, but the Spirit who is from God, that we might know the things that have been freely given to us by God...Go and manifest to your world – unleash the lion within.*

Discover the secrets about your assignment hidden away in the secret treasury of Heaven. You are a lion in the order of Christ, so roar in prayer and get ready to tear to shreds the fake lions of this world. I would like to sound a note of warning at this point to all those walking by assumptions. Assumptions can be deadly - the Bible says the Lord knows those who are His – as a Lion, He has many sons who are lions too because like begets like. Don't assume anything today. If you are not yet saved, confronting the lions of this world could be very dangerous. Make sure you settle the question of salvation in your life before anything else so you don't become the hunted like the account of the impersonators recorded in **Acts 19:14-16.**

It is time to pray!

DAY 10 PRAYER POINTS

1. Thank You Lord for saving me and striking all my enemies on the cheekbone. Thank You for breaking the teeth of the wicked on my behalf.

2. Thank You Lord for making me into a new threshing instrument with sharp teeth. Thank You for transforming me daily into the image of the LION OF JUDAH.

3. Thank You Lord for Your enabling grace to continue in this 21 days journey of transfiguration. Thank You for my life and my family.

4. Father Lord baptize me afresh with the spirit of boldness; let my faith increase as I dwell daily at Your temple and feast daily at Your table. I eat strong meat and I enjoy the honey of Your word in Jesus' name.

5. From today, let me operate the anointing of a king and the boldness of a lion. As the righteous of the Lord, I am bold and refuse to turn back from adverse situations or demonic afflictions in Jesus' name. I set the captives free!

6. The Lion within me arise! I operate with uncommon stamina in the place of fasting and prayer; as a son of the Lion of Judah, the Root of David I am empowered to tear the lions of wickedness to pieces in Jesus' name.

7. From today, I enjoy the lion-share in life; I will no longer eat left-over crumbs like dogs. I am head and not tail, above only and not beneath in Jesus' name. I am a fore-runner at work and in school, at home and abroad!

8. As a lion of the Most High and a son of the LION OF JUDAH, I defy every ancestral lions and trample down every territorial lion of wickedness in Jesus' name. I silence

every roaring of the devourer and arrest every activity of darkness in my family!

9. I will not lack any good thing and my children will not suffer hunger; before we call for help a thousand will respond and before we look for food our storehouses will be filled with all manner of provisions in Jesus' name.

10. **COMMUNION:** Father Lord, baptize me afresh with the spirit of boldness and give me the heart of a lion. When others fear, let me rise with faith and where other people fail, let me excel exceedingly in Jesus' mighty name.

Give thanks for answered prayer!

INSTRUCTION: Get up at the midnight watch and roar like a lion at that problem that stared you in the face for so long - PRAY IN THE SPIRIT FOR 30 MINUTES.

DAY 11
GLORY OF GOD AND KINGS

Today is the eleventh day of the fast and we see from **Genesis 37** that Joseph the son of Jacob operated by the spirit of revelation in dreams; he knew things ahead of time and saw things before they happened. My prayer for you is that as you pursue the Lord God on this Mountain of Transfiguration, you will begin to see into the spirit realm and know things before they happen in Jesus' name. You will not be stranded in life anymore and you will excel with the anointing of ease where others are struggling because of the divine secrets available to you. The Bible says in the book of **Proverbs 25:2,**

It is the glory of God to conceal a matter, But the glory of kings is to search out a matter.

God has secrets and it is clear from scriptures that He shares it with whosoever He chooses. He is a super mysterious God who can hide in darkness to confound the enemy,

Psalm 18:11,

He made darkness His secret place; His canopy around Him was dark waters And thick clouds of the skies.

I have experienced His overwhelming presence in very dark situations before. He hides me in the shadow of His wings all the time. And there is a place called His secret pavilion according to **Psalm 27:5**,

> *For in the time of trouble He shall hide me in His pavilion; In the secret place of His tabernacle He shall hide me; He shall set me high upon a rock.*

Especially on those days when the forces of darkness will not stop threatening, the Lord will hide you from evil. **Psalm 31:20** says,

> *You shall hide them in the secret place of Your presence From the plots of man; You shall keep them secretly in a pavilion From the strife of tongues.*

This God has a place called the secret place of thunder according to **Psalm 81:7**, *You called in trouble, and I delivered you; I answered you in the secret place of thunder; I tested you at the waters of Meribah.* He can also lead you into immense wealth and treasure if you pay attention to His invaluable secrets as recorded in **Isaiah 45:3**,

> *I will give you the treasures of darkness And hidden riches of secret places, That you may know that I, the Lord, Who call you by your name, Am the God of Israel.*

Psalm 25:14 says,

> *The secret of the Lord is with those who fear Him, And He will show them His covenant.*

Remember when a sentence was released to kill all the wise men in the book of Daniel because a king slept and dreamt but when he woke up, had forgotten his dream, but the secret was revealed to Daniel in a night vision (Daniel 2:19-22).

THERE IS A GOD WHO REVEALS SECRETS!

But who are those He reveals these secrets to? **Amos 3:7** says,

> *Surely the Lord God does nothing, Unless He reveals His secret to His servants the prophets.*

A prophet is one who prays and seeks Him on the watchtower night and day engaging the prayer watches. If you search the scriptures properly, you will find out that those who seek Him usually find Him and His secret. The easiest place to discover His secret is in His word and through prayer.

We can see that from the main text of this fast in **Luke 9:29-37 (The Voice)**,

> *Jesus began to pray and the disciples tried to stay awake, but their eyes grew heavier and heavier and finally they all fell asleep. When they awakened, they looked over at Jesus and saw something inexplicable happening. Jesus was changing before their eyes, beginning with His face. It seemed to glow. The glow spread, and even His clothing took on a blinding whiteness. Then, two figures appeared in the glorious radiance emanating from Jesus.*

> *The three disciples somehow knew that these figures were Moses and Elijah. Peter, James, and John overheard the conversation that took place among Jesus, Moses, and Elijah—a conversation that centered on Jesus' "departure" and how He would accomplish this departure from the capital city, Jerusalem. The glow began to fade, and it was clear that Moses and Elijah were about to disappear. Peter said to Jesus: Please, Master, it is good for us to be here and see this. Can we make three structures—one to honor You, one to honor Moses, and one to honor Elijah, to try to capture what's happening here? Peter had no idea what he was saying. While he*

spoke a cloud descended, and they were enveloped in it, and fear fell on them. Then a voice came out of everywhere and nowhere at once. Voice from Heaven: This is My Son! This is the One I have chosen! Listen to Him! Then the voice was silent, the cloud disappeared, and Moses and Elijah were gone. Peter, James, and John were left speechless, stunned, staring at Jesus who now stood before them alone. For a long time, they did not say a word about this whole experience. They came down the mountain, and the next day yet another huge crowd gathered around Jesus. There was even a man in the crowd who shouted out.

Don't you realize that nothing catches God by surprise? He knows all things and that is why we call Him OMNISCIENT GOD! All-knowing God. Jesus actually went to the mountain to discuss His exit from the earth. He went to His Father for the details. Why don't you seek His opinion about that next step? Why don't you seek His face about that situation? He already knows what all the wise men on the earth know or what any prophet will ever reveal to you for that matter. He was the one who revealed it to them in the first place.

As a son of God, why don't you ask your heavenly Father about what the rest of this year holds for you? As an intercessor on the tower, why don't you watch to see what He will say concerning that family, nation or generation? He is your Maker; why don't you ask what He had in mind when He created you? He is ready to share those deep secrets if only you are willing to seek Him. Did you know that you were the king the Bible was referring to in that scripture? **Proverbs 25:2** says, *It is the glory of God to conceal a matter, But the glory of kings is to search out a matter.* The Bible says you have been made kings and priests unto our God. He calls you a royal priesthood - do you now get it? Royal - you are a king, priesthood - you are a priest. Hallelujah! You need to switch from regular mode to supernatural mode; you need to move from casual mode to intelligent mode where you will be alert in the spirit with supernatural intelligence!

The two men that appeared on the Mountain of Transfiguration (Moses and Elijah) operated by divine secrets throughout their ministry on the earth. Especially when their assignment was done, God told them when they will be taken and how to prepare. Moses knew when he would be taken in **Deuteronomy 32:48-50**, *Then the Lord spoke to Moses that very same day, saying: "Go up this mountain of the Abarim, Mount Nebo, ... and die on the mountain which you ascend, and be gathered to your people...* He anointed a successor in his place. **Deuteronomy 34:9** says that Joshua the son of Nun was full of the spirit of wisdom, because Moses had laid his hands on him. The same was with Elijah; he knew when he was about to be taken. 2 Kings 2:1, *And it came to pass, when the Lord was about to take up Elijah into heaven by a whirlwind, that Elijah went with Elisha from Gilgal and he also anointed Elisha in his place.*

Jesus knew when He will be taken and He also anointed His successors with double portion of His anointing first in John 20:22 when He breathed on them and said to them, Receive the Holy Spirit and again on the day of Pentecost. From today, you will no longer be afraid of what ordinary men are afraid of and you will not die anyhow in Jesus' name! Neither will you fall like one of the princes! Jesus actually went up on the Mountain of Transfiguration to discuss His exit. He did not approach it any how. He did not avoid or ignore it. He went to praying and fasting - He engaged the prayer of inquiry. Do you know you have what it takes? **Job 32:8** says that *there is a spirit in man, And the breath of the Almighty gives him understanding.*

The Holy Spirit is the greatest Help when it comes to unraveling the secrets of God.

1 Corinthians 2:9-12,

> But as it is written:"Eye has not seen, nor ear heard,Nor have entered into the heart of man The things which God has prepared for those who love Him." But God has revealed them to us through His Spirit. For the Spirit searches all things, yes, the deep things of God. For what man knows the things of a man except the spirit of the man which is in him? Even so no one knows the things of God except the Spirit of God. Now we have received, not the spirit of the world, but the Spirit who is from God, that we might know the things that have been freely given to us by God.

THE SECRET IS ONLY ACCESSIBLE TO THOSE WHO ARE SAVED! The scripture we just read makes it clear that the unsaved mind cannot discern the secrets with the natural mind.

1 Corinthians 2:13-14,

> These things we also speak, not in words which man's wisdom teaches but which the Holy Spirit teaches, comparing spiritual things with spiritual. But the natural man does not receive the things of the Spirit of God, for they are foolishness to him; nor can he know them, because they are spiritually discerned.

Do you want to operate by supernatural intelligence, enjoying the secret treasures stowed away before the foundation of the world? Then you need to acquaint yourself with the Father of Spirits. You need to befriend Jesus! You need learn all the secrets from Him. He is the only way, the legitimate door and the key to accessing God's secret pavilion. Ask the Holy Spirit for help, He is the revealer of secrets. You are king and a priest of the Most High God, you can access the glory that belongs to God and kings.

It is time to pray!

DAY 11 PRAYER POINTS

1. Thank You Lord for the spirit within me giving me understanding and showing me secrets by your inspiration. Thank You Lord for counting me worthy!

2. Thank You Father for not allowing me to get the judgement I deserve but trading my sins with the righteousness of Christ Jesus on the cross of Calvary.

3. Thank You Lord for the Mountain of Transfiguration; these past few days have been so empowering and life transforming! Thank You for your mercy and grace.

4. Father Lord, grant me access to the secrets that will showcase your glory in my life this year. Let me operate your divine intelligence for the remaining months of this year in Jesus' name.

5. From today, Lord I enter the secret place of your pavilion through prayer and praise. I tap into your secret treasures through Your word and meditation in Jesus' name.

6. Lord, as I go higher on this Mountain of Transfiguration envelope me with Your pillar of cloud by day and your pillar of fire by night. Answer me from the secret place of thunder as I confront the secrets of my father's house and my mother's house.

7. Father Lord, reveal to me the secret details of my assignment and show me the secret of my generation, so that I can

effectively fulfill my purpose in Christ Jesus. Help me to raise other lions for your kingdom!

8. Lord, lead me to discover the secret treasures of darkness and the hidden riches of secret places. As I pray through the night watches, open eyes to see deep secrets and as I engage the early watch open my ears to hear great mysteries in Jesus' name.

9. By the secrets I contact on this mountain of transfiguration, I will emerge a transformer to my world at the end of the 21 days fasting and prayer. No more struggling with dreams and interpretation - I operate with vision and precision in Jesus' name.

10. COMMUNION: Father Lord, anoint me afresh with the spirit of wisdom and revelation in the knowledge of You. I will not die like men nor fall like one of the princes - I walk in the fullness of the days assigned to me and, like Jesus, I enjoy the details of my exit when my assignment is done.

INSTRUCTION: At the midnight watch ask the Lord for something He wants you to do for Him before the year is over. Write it down and run with it - He will surprise you with a divine exchange like Solomon and Hannah.

DAY 12

DESTINY, COME FORTH

Today is the twelfth day and the number 12 represents divine order and governance. There were 12 disciples, there are 12 tribes of Israel, there are 12 hours in a day like the Master said in (**John 11:9**); a new day starts at 12 midnight (so does a new month and a new year), there are 12 months in a year. From today, your life will follow divine order in Jesus' name.

Revelation 21:10-14,

And he carried me away in the Spirit to a great and high mountain, and showed me the great city, the holy Jerusalem, descending out of heaven from God, having the glory of God. Her light was like a most precious stone, like a jasper stone, clear as crystal. Also she had a great and high wall with twelve gates, and twelve angels at the gates, and names written on them, which are the names of the twelve tribes of the children of Israel: three gates on the east, three gates on the north, three gates on the south, and three gates on the west. Now the wall of the city had twelve foundations, and on them were the names of the twelve apostles of the Lamb.

Your life will bear fruits for each month of this year like the tree mentioned in **Revelation 22:1-2**. You will receive more than you ever bargained for from the throne room of God because you are on this mountain. Your life will follow divine order from today in Jesus' name! Your destiny will align to its divine mandate from the Orchestrator of Destinies! I decree that your destiny must come forth.

You can see how the Lord called forth a dead destiny in **John 11:1**, *Now a certain man was sick, Lazarus of Bethany, the town of Mary and her sister Martha. Verse 6. So, when He heard that he was sick, He stayed two more days in the place where He was.*

I truly believe our Lord was praying about the situation when He stayed for two more days and He referred to this prayer at the tomb in **John 11:41-44**,

> *Then they took away the stone from the place where the dead man was lying. And Jesus lifted up His eyes and said, "Father, I thank You that* ***You have heard Me.*** *And I know that You always hear Me, but because of the people who are standing by I said this, that they may believe that You sent Me." Now when He had said these things, He CRIED WITH A LOUD VOICE, "Lazarus, come forth!" And he who had died came out bound hand and foot with grave clothes, and his face was wrapped with a cloth. Jesus said to them, "Loose him, and let him go."*

Lazarus had lost his name, his life and calling. His destiny was erased! He no longer had an identity but was simply referred to as the dead man. Even his sister did not use his name anymore. His destiny suspended! How many have lost their identities? How many have lost the true meaning of life – I speak to every lost destiny; be restored back to the master's plan now in

Jesus' name! Do you know that you are here on the earth for the Master's errand, not your own? The best person to ask for help is the One who sent you here; He will back you up. Like Lazarus, many destinies are dead, many destinies have been shut up behind the stone. Rotting away in the tomb of decay, but praise be to God, help is available today.

When Jesus showed up, Lazarus' destiny was restored! When the RESURRECTION AND THE LIFE showed up on the scene, He called him by name - LAZARUS, come forth! His name means GOD'S HELP - Jesus, his helper, called out his destiny. He addressed his assignment, He restored His calling! The One who molded his destiny, gave him back what the devil stole! He called out HELP, come forth! Help is available for you today. Your enemy may think that Help is far from you. The enemy is in for a shock because HELP is on the way. HELP is never late; your HELP is here now!

I wonder what type of sickness killed him. The Bible never mentioned the nature of the affliction but he was set free from the sickness when the Great Physician called him out – He addressed his health. The spirit of infirmity was shattered! The spirit of death was disgraced. The grave had to bow out to the One who holds the key of life and death! The grave had no choice but to spit him up! Today, that health problem regardless of the name will not escape the Master's attention! Imagine if you will: Lazarus was dead for four days already. He was stinking! The maggots would have been feasting ceaselessly; the worms would have had their own fair share. The grave rats would have bitten out their pound of flesh. O what a sight it must have been! His genes had decomposed; his entire blood drained. The Bible says the life of the flesh is the blood - so life was drained from him. His DNA was rendered inactive.

In his gene and DNA was his dominion, hegemony, mastery, power, command, rulership, sway, authority, governance, his possession and territory. He lost relevance; his staff of bread taken forever. His Success fizzled out. He was brain dead. His passions and emotions, forgotten. His dreams erased! His aspirations deleted! He never got to be a husband; he never got to become a father. He went to the grave barren!

There was no mention of his wife or children so that meant his marital destiny was also sick, dead and stinking but I believe, the Master addressed his marriage that day. He got a fresh start and a brand new beginning. You will get a new beginning today! This God is able to revive dead wombs and visit dead situations! No matter how dead your situation is, the Resurrection and Life can reverse it in a heartbeat. The Lord just opened His mouth and death gave up Lazarus. Knowing that the One he could not refuse had come! When he spoke, every dead cell came alive! Death gave way to life. When he spoke all the rottenness left and fresh life came. When He spoke, the maggots and worms that were having a feast on the body of Lazarus gave up what they had eaten. When he uttered His voice every sting of the death and chains of the grave gave way! His words went back in time to restore Lazarus to a state of perfection! His destiny was restored!

Like Lazarus, be restored back to your destiny in Christ Jesus! He boldly addressed death and defeated the grave at the tomb of Lazarus. He called forth the lost destiny with authority. How? He had mastered the flesh. He had silenced the flesh through fasting, so He was operating in the Spirit. He did miracles seamlessly and addressed demons sweat-lessly. I can tell you that the secret of His boldness was from the mountain experience. He spent a lot of time in prayer and fasting. He was in constant touch with the Father. He was empowered so much because he knew how to deal with the flesh and let out the spirit. Peter, John and James may have seen it once on the Mountain of Transfiguration but I believe that it was a regular occurrence whenever our Lord Jesus prayed.

Look again at **Luke 9:28-29**, *Now it came to pass, about eight days after these sayings, that He took Peter, John, and James and went up on the mountain to pray. As He prayed, the appearance of His face was altered, and His robe became white and glistening. He was transformed before their very eyes.* From this season of fasting, you will be transformed into your true nature. You will manifest as a god on the earth and a terror to the kingdom of darkness. Your destiny will be released majestically in Jesus' name.

Jesus had been fasting and praying on the mountain as was his habit. He was able to unleash His divine nature every time He engaged this divine secret. That was why He stayed two more days when he heard Lazarus was sick - He stayed to pray! We are just like Him and we are able to manifest our true nature as we spend time looking at the mirror of His word. The secret of Jesus' earthly ministry was His constant communion with the Father. He raised the dead and destroyed demonic yokes while constantly replenishing His anointing in the place of prayer and fasting.

Applying this scripture in our case today, we can call any yoke Lazarus; whatever delay you are experiencing is Lazarus, the marital problem is Lazarus, and you represent Jesus Christ – because as He is so are we in this world. We are His ambassadors and so we must walk like He walked, demonstrating His power and authority over demonic afflictions, diseases and death. So like Jesus Christ, you must look at the dead situations, the stagnated destiny and that life-calling that has been lying fallow and you will call it forth. You must call forth that destiny that is bound hand and foot, it is time for a divine release – you must work the works of Him who sent you here. You must run your particular race in destiny! You must proclaim – DESTINY, COME FORTH!!

It is time to pray!

DAY 12 PRAYER POINTS

1. Thank You Lord for the beauty of another day in Your presence. Thank You for bringing me to the twelfth day of this fast. Thank You Lord for the revelation knowledge You have given me from this altar of prayer.

2. Thank You for the hand of protection over me and my family throughout this year. Thank You for sending me help from Your sanctuary and for hiding me in the shadow of Your wings.

3. Thank You Lord for showing me the secrets of my destiny and for sending me here with a divine mandate.

4. Resurrection and the Life fight all my dark battles - The generational battles from my father's house, my mother's house and through marriage (sickness, failure, untimely death, poverty, shame, birth defect, like father like son syndrome etc.)

5. Resurrection and the Life, show up for me in this matter: _____ mention the area before the Lord. Revive my marriage, womb, career, business, academics, finances, ministry

etc. Let the dry bones live again! Reverse every evil report!

6. My destiny, come forth! My star arise! Receive the anointing to excel in Jesus' name. Come out of the tomb of non-achievement and stagnation. You were made for greatness!

7. No evil shall befall me or my household because the law of the Spirit of Life is at work in me. I shall not die but live to declare the glory of the Lord in the land of the living.

8. I have a blood covenant with Christ Jesus, and shatter the power of untimely death; nothing is permitted to die around me anymore because greater is He that is in me than he that is in the world.

9. I have the same Spirit that raised Christ from the dead; my body is quickened for my assignment. My soul receives the baptism of fire —y anointing to fast and pray, fall upon me. I am empowered as an intercessor to lift up my voice on behalf of others.

12. COMMUNION: God of perfection, perfect that which concerns me. Let my life follow divine order from today. Let this year yield its fruits for my entire household. I have authority and manifest greatness!

Give thanks for answered prayer!

INSTRUCTION: At the midnight watch ask the Lord for the details of your destiny. Ask Him to revisit any lost vision and restore lost dreams. Speak to your destiny to come forth in Jesus' name!

DAY 13

ELECTRIFIED

Today is the thirteenth day of the fast and in **Luke 13:13**, we see that Jesus laid hands on the woman with the spirit of infirmity and immediately she was made straight, glorifying God. I pray that today you will receive the electrifying touch of Jesus that will turn you to a powerhouse for His glory. You will be transformed by His power to become a mighty transformer in your generation. I pray that your prayer life will become super-charged with the power of the Most High God this season! You will shine as light in the darkness of this world in Jesus' matchless name.

From the Mountain of Transfiguration, we can see the electrifying effect of prayer and fasting in the life of the Master.

Luke 9:29,
> *And as He was praying, the appearance of His countenance became altered different, and His raiment became dazzling white flashing with the brilliance of lightning.*

And the two men who were there with him at the top of the mountain were Moses and Elijah, those icons of the faith, beloved of God. And they talked to Jesus. Remember that I said previously that these men did not appear by accident; in their lifetime on the earth, they had both experienced God in many similar ways. They were a type or a shadow of what was to come - both men had experienced the supernatural and walked in miraculous exploits in their ministry. They both had the unique testimony of having fasted for 40 days and forty nights without food or water.

For instance, I love the glimpse of God's light bulb that Moses saw in the wilderness in **Exodus 3:2**,

> *The Angel of the Lord appeared to him in a flame of fire out of the midst of a bush; and he looked, and behold, the bush burned with fire, yet was not consumed.*

The tree radiated light without being burnt - isn't this light similar to the invention of Thomas Edison in the form of the incandescent light bulb that shines in billions of homes all over the world? The light bulb did not originate from Edison, it came from the Light Himself. You can tap into that same grace of invention of global magnitude and generational impact. The Bible also records that Moses had the same glory radiating from his face after he came down from the mountain of the Lord, such that no one could look him in the face (**Exodus 34:28-29**).

Moses was there with the Lord forty days and forty nights; he ate no bread and drank no water. And he wrote upon the tables the words of the covenant, the Ten Commandments. When Moses came down from Mount Sinai with the two tables of the Testimony in his hand, he did not know that the skin of his face shone and sent forth beams of light by reason of his spending time with the Lord.

Notice that the Bible records the same concerning our Savior, His face glowed and his robe became dazzling white with the flashing brilliance of lightning. He was emanating with power, he was radiating with divine energy. No wonder He carried the power that could transform lives in an instant! He touched many lives and healed the sick with the instant effect and speed of light. Jesus was a POWERHOUSE and so are we. The Bible mentions that the same power is at work in us in **Ephesians 3:20,**

> *Now to Him who is able to do exceedingly abundantly above all that we ask or think, according to the* ***power*** *that works in us.*

This is also repeated in **Ephesians 1:19,**

> *And what is the exceeding greatness of His* ***power*** *toward us who believe, according to the working of His mighty* ***power****.*

This power could not keep him dead - **Ephesians 1:20,** *which He worked in Christ when He raised Him from the dead and seated Him at His right hand in the heavenly places.*

The Bible confirms that we carry this same power – the power that raises the dead.

Romans 8:11,

> *But if the Spirit of Him who raised Jesus from the dead dwells in you, He who raised Christ from the dead will also give life to your mortal bodies through His Spirit who dwells in you.*

In the physical, power can flow in form of electricity. Power is also known as dynamo or what the Bible refers to as *dunamis* in Greek. Electricity gives out such effects as lightning, static electricity and electric current. Power generators and transformers are used to transmit electricity with high voltage. You are like that power generator or transformer – you must serve your generation as a power distribution center like our Master Jesus. **Psalm 62:11** declares, *"God has spoken once, Twice I have heard this: that power belongs to God".* This power electrocutes demons; no wonder Jesus dealt with the demon that the disciples could not handle in the boy. Jesus had given the disciples this same power in **Matthew 10:1,**

> *And when He had called His twelve disciples to Him, He gave them power over unclean spirits, to cast them out, and to heal all kinds of sickness and all kinds of disease.*

And the same is confirmed in **Luke 9:1-2,**

> *Then He called His twelve disciples together and gave them power and authority over all demons, and to cure diseases. He sent them to preach the kingdom of God and to heal the sick.*

The only problem with them at the time was that they had not yet mastered this power or maintain the flow through fasting and prayer according to **Matthew 17:21.**

Jesus spoke about dealing ancestral scorpions and age-old serpents with this power in **Luke 10:19,**

> *Behold, I give you the authority to trample on serpents and scorpions, and over all the power of the enemy, and nothing shall by any means hurt you.*

This power changes men and brings them to complete repentance according to **Luke 1:16-17**. This power can overshadow a woman and make her pregnant instantly without any man involved in the process according to **Luke 1:35**. Jesus was a powerhouse and his robes, voice, and shadow were conduits of this electrifying power. **Luke 6:19** records that the whole multitude sought to touch Him, for power went out from Him and healed them all. This was the same electric flow of power that healed the woman with the issue of blood when she touched His robe in **Luke 8:46**. The Holy Spirit is our source of this electric power today. The Bible says in **Acts 1:8**,

> *But you shall receive power when the Holy Spirit has come upon you; and you shall be witnesses to Me in Jerusalem, and in all Judea and Samaria, and to the end of the earth."*

This was the same spirit that anointed Jesus for exploits according to **Acts 10:38**,

> *How God anointed Jesus of Nazareth with the Holy Spirit and with power, who went about doing good and healing all who were oppressed by the devil, for God was with Him.*

He also appeared as a mighty rushing wind of fire on the Day of Pentecost, infusing the disciples as generational transformers in **Acts 2:1-4**. As a representative of the Lord on the earth, you need to tap into this Power Source. After He comes upon you, this power destroys fear according to **2 Timothy 1:7**. With this power, you can start operating at a higher level of supernatural exploits, defeating sickness and destroying strongholds. God uses this power in form of lightning bolts and thunder to destroy the enemy.

2 Samuel 22:14-15,

> *The Lord thundered from heaven, and the Most High uttered His voice. He sent out arrows and scattered them; lightning confused and troubled them.*

You need to understand that this power is only released and distributed through passion and compassion.

Matthew 14:14,

When Jesus went out He saw a great multitude; and He was moved with compassion for them, and healed their sick. It was this compassion that released this power to the multitude.

As a powerhouse, you can stir up this **dunamis** by the same key. You can also unleash this electrifying power through passionate prayer like the prophet Elijah according to **James 5:16b-18,**

The earnest heartfelt, continued prayer of a righteous man makes tremendous power available dynamic in its working. Elijah was a human being with a nature such as we have with feelings, affections, and a constitution like ours; and he prayed earnestly for it not to rain, and no rain fell on the earth for three years and six months. And then he prayed again and the heavens supplied rain and the land produced its crops as usual.

Paul taught Timothy how to stir up this dynamic working power through praying, especially praying in the spirit in **2 Timothy 1:6,**

Therefore I remind you to stir up the gift of God which is in you through the laying on of my hands.

You can have an electrified prayer life that can release thunderbolts and lighting from heaven if you just key in properly during this 21 days of fasting and prayer – you can see the effect of the prayers of the saints in heaven from **Revelation 8:3-5,**

Then another angel, having a golden censer, came and stood at the altar. He was given much incense, that he should offer it with the prayers of all the saints upon the golden altar which was before the throne. And the smoke of the incense, with the prayers of the saints, ascended before God from the angel's hand. Then the angel took the censer, filled it with fire from the altar, and threw it to the earth. And there were noises, thunderings, lightnings, and an earthquake.

There is a secret that most people are scared of and it is fasting and prayer. Many fear fasting because they do not the power latent within. The latent force in your spirit is unleashed and made potent through fasting and prayer. Fasting without praying is lame and it is just hunger strike. But fasting according to the word of God empowers you; it electrifies you just like what **Isaiah 40:29-31** says.

When you abstain from food ordinarily, you get weak and tired but when you add prayer, labor in the word and praise through to breakthrough, it is electrifying! It charges your spirit man with fire. The word of God electrifies you; it is better than radiation or laser focus; it penetrates where the medical gadgets cannot reach and runs deeper than any surgical blade according to **Hebrews 4:12**. You can defeat cancer with this electrifying power. You can burn up the spirit of infirmity with this power. You must walk this side of eternity as a transformer and an effective power center transmitting healing to the sick and setting the captives free.

It is time to pray!

DAY 13 PRAYER POINTS

1. Thank You Lord for this beautiful day of worship and fellowship. Thank You for the gift of life and family.

2. Thank You Lord for calling me out as a lighthouse and a power center. Thank You for the fresh revelation on this mountain of transfiguration.

3. Thank You Lord for the empowering journey of the last few days in Your presence. Thank You for increasing my strength and renewing my stamina like the eagles.

4. Father Lord, anoint me with the Holy Spirit and power like Jesus; let my shadow heal the sick and let me voice frighten demons out of their hide-outs. I operate with the passion and compassion that releases Your power.

5. From this mountain, cause me to contact the electrifying power in Your word. Let my prayers compel lightning and let my praise command a thunderstorm. Move me by Your Spirit so I can move my world in Jesus' name.

6. From today, I handle the sword of the Spirit with authority to shatter cancer, fibriomyalgia, HIV, Lupus, diabetes, down syndrome, insanity, arthritis, birth defects and all manner of diseases troubling my generation. I AM A POWER-CENTER!

7. Like Moses, touch my prayer altar with your power and rain down your fire on me like prophet Elijah of old. Let the world see your glory radiating like flashes of lightning from my life in Jesus' name.

8. Lord, strengthen me and infuse me with your Spirit of love, power and boldness. Let me operate with the authority

of my Lord Jesus; quicken my spirit, soul and body with resurrection power!

9. Today, I take authority over territorial forces of darkness and disgrace every ancestral serpent. I shatter every covenant of household wickedness impacting my health, marriage, academics or destiny by the blood of Jesus. NO MORE MANIPULATION!

10. COMMUNION: Baptize me with power to change my world for your glory. Move me from the realm of talking to the realm of power that cannot be insulted by this communion table.

Give thanks for answered prayer!

INSTRUCTION: At the midnight watch address one issue before the Lord that is about you and address two for other people that are close to you: sow an uncommon seed for financial breakthrough.

DAY 14

DOUBLE PERFECTION

Today is the fourteenth day of the fast and we know that the number seven represents perfection and rest. It is the Lord's Sabbath. The Sabbath represents rest from all labor – No more struggling, no more toiling and no more labor! Your work will become something of joy and fulfillment in the name of Jesus. God worked and enjoyed it thoroughly; you will not cease enjoying the fruit of your work in Jesus' name. The Sabbath also represents the day of absolute worship to the Lord – a day where you hallow the name of the Lord, a day dedicated to praising and honoring Him, a day where all those who love the Lord have chosen to honor and reverence Him.

I have personally decided to have a sabbatical attitude all the days of my life. It is an attitude of gratitude, an atmosphere of praise, an environment of glory and beauty. The Bible says in His presence is fullness of joy and at His right hands pleasures forever more (**Psalm 16:11**). You can create that attitude of praise that will open the heavens permanently over your head.

The beauty of today is that we have the number 14 in it – it means that we will enjoy double rest and double perfection! The Lord has commanded a rest from all labor for you; from today you will enter into your season of unending supply—

perfection in the works of your hands, perfection in your finances. You will learn how to provoke divine rest and how to sustain it permanently. You will be learning the secret of praying and singing scriptures. Praise songs that are taken directly from scriptures. You can sing songs like, "Forever, O Lord your word is settled in heaven, it is settled" (**Psalm 119:89 NKJV**). Another one is "Great is the Lord and greatly to be praised, in the city of the Lord, in the mountain of His holiness. Beautiful for situation, the joy of the whole world… (**Psalm 48:1, 2 NKJV**). Did you know that many songs written in the Bible are also sung in heaven? Many warfare songs like, "Let God arise, let His enemies be scattered" (**Psalm 68:1 NKJV**) and many others written all through the scriptures? If I were you, I will learn as many of them as I possibly could.

We have established that God inhabits the praises of His people. When praises go up, His glory comes down. We have also seen from scriptures that when our prayer goes up, His fire falls like rain. We know that when we pray according to His will He hears us (**1 John 5:14**) – that means there is a proper way to pray. **James 4:2-4** also talks about praying amiss. Brethren, I can tell you with confidence that God answers prayers and there is no ritual or tradition to it. It is simply laid out for us to see in scriptures. When you pray according to His will about any matter and when His desire coincides with your desire, then you are guaranteed answered prayers! His will is His word!

How come Moses got answers every time he prayed or Elijah got answers with God's audible voice? How come Jesus also got all His petition granted? Even when it was a tough assignment or a bitter pill to swallow, He always heard back from the Father clearly. I am happy to announce to you that there is a proper way to praise God and move heaven. It is also laid out for us in scriptures.

Jesus is the Lion of the Tribe of Judah (praise): He is also known as the Root of David. The tabernacle that God chose to dwell forever is that of David. Why? Because David knew how to praise Him. **Acts 13:22** says it this way,

He raised up for them David as king, to whom also He gave testimony and said, 'I have found David the son of Jesse, a man after My own heart, who will do all My will.'

What is His will here? PRAISE! David wrote many songs that were divinely inspired by God, many of the songs we still sing today without knowing. The angelic choir are singing the same! When we sing in unison with the heavenly choir, you can be sure that the glory cloud will descend.

When Solomon and the children of Israel were dedicating the temple in **2 Chronicles 5:13-14**, HIS GLORY CLOUD FILLED THE HOUSE just like the cloud descended on the Mountain of Transfiguration with Jesus,

"Indeed it came to pass, when the trumpeters and singers were as one, to make one sound to be heard in praising and thanking the Lord, and when they lifted up their voice with the trumpets and cymbals and instruments of music, and praised the Lord, saying: "For He is good, For His mercy endures forever," that the house, the house of the Lord, was filled with a cloud, so that the priests could not continue ministering because of the cloud; for the glory of the Lord filled the house of God."

The cloud is the physical manifestation of Divine Presence. It also happened with Moses, he was used to walking in and out of the glory clouds. The same happened with Elijah so much so that he was eventually taken up in the glory clouds when he was leaving the earth.

From today, as you engage the mystery of singing and praying scriptures, may you experience His glory clouds forever! May the abiding presence of God be with you everywhere you go in Jesus' name. May heaven's provision be forever open everywhere you reside on the face of the earth. May you enjoy double perfection in every area of your life. Moses wrote several songs in scriptures. One is recorded in **Exodus 15:1-19**; he sang a song when the Lord swallowed up Pharaoh and his army in the Red Sea. In **Deuteronomy 31:19** - The Lord instructed Moses,

> *Now therefore, write down this song for yourselves, and teach it to the children of Israel; put it in their mouths, that this song may be a witness for Me against the children of Israel.* ²² *Therefore Moses wrote this song the same day, and taught it to the children of Israel.*

You can find the song in **Deuteronomy 32:1-44**. For eternity the songs of Moses are being sung in heaven - and the glory cloud is still showing up. Where did you think he got the songs from in the first place? He was inspired from above!

See **Revelation 15:3-8,**

> *"They sing the song of Moses, the servant of God, and the song of the Lamb, saying: "Great and marvelous are Your works, Lord God Almighty! Just and true are Your ways, O King of the saints! Who shall not fear You, O Lord, and glorify Your name? For You alone are holy. For all nations shall come and worship before You, For Your judgments have been manifested." After these things I looked, and behold, the temple of the tabernacle of the testimony in heaven was opened. And out of the temple came the seven angels having the seven plagues, clothed in pure bright linen, and having their chests girded with golden bands. Then one of the four living creatures gave to the seven angels seven golden*

bowls full of the wrath of God who lives forever and ever. The temple was filled with smoke from the glory of God and from His power, and no one was able to enter the temple till the seven plagues of the seven angels were completed."

Did you notice that the temple in heaven was filled with smoke? True worship provokes divine presence. Time will fail us to look at some others who sang and prayed scriptures. Hannah and Mary sang scriptures; they both got their babies –

Hannah: 1 Samuel 2:1-3 *"And Hannah prayed and said: "My heart rejoices in the Lord; My horn is exalted in the Lord. I smile at my enemies, Because I rejoice in Your salvation. "No one is holy like the Lord, For there is none besides You, Nor is there any rock like our God. "Talk no more so very proudly; Let no arrogance come from your mouth, For the Lord is the God of knowledge; And by Him actions are weighed."*

Mary: Luke 1:46-47 *And Mary said:"My soul magnifies the Lord, And my spirit has rejoiced in God my Savior.*

Daniel sang in Daniel 2:19-23; Miriam sang, Jehoshaphat and the list goes on. The Sons of Korah wrote many psalms and so did David and Solomon. They were written for our example, divinely inspired so that we know how to sing and pray scriptures. Many of these songs are being sung in heaven as we speak. You can also receive the grace to tap into heaven's wavelength as you journey on in this fast. Like I said when you key into this level of perfection in prayer and praise, you will become a world shaker and a kingdom mover. You will emerge at the foot of this Mountain of Transfiguration not only transformed but as a TRANSFORMER to your world!

It is time for us to pray.

DAY 14 PRAYER POINTS

1. Thank you Lord for this day of divine rest and double perfection. Thank you for your unfailing love and mercy toward me.

2. Thank you for this Mountain of Transfiguration, revelation and elevation. Thank you for showing me the secret of sabbatical rest.

3. Thank you Lord for my assignment on the earth; I am forever grateful for showing me how to provoke the glory clouds through prayer and praise.

4. Father Lord, anoint me to sing and pray according to scriptures like the men of old. Move me from the outer courts to the inner sanctuary of your presence. Let me hear you audibly from today in Jesus' name.

5. As I pray scriptures and praise according to your will, let the earth yield her increase for me. Let your glory cloud descend over my household and let the chains of brass and fetters of iron be shattered forever in Jesus' name!

6. According to the revelation on this mountain, I no longer pray amiss or praise in the flesh. I pray and sing scriptures like Moses; I sing heaven's chorus and I write inspired songs for God's glory in Jesus' name.

7. As I operate the mystery of prayer and praise, my life will shock my enemies and surprise my friends. They will be stunned and amazed at my testimonies from this mountain of transfiguration in Jesus' name.

8. As I lift up the name of Jesus all men will come unto Him! As I praise the name of the Lord, I am raised up from zero to hero. As I honor Him, He will honor me. As I shout His praise,

He will announce me to my world as a son of the Most High!

9. I am for miracle, signs and wonders! My life is a reflection of God's glory and I operate by supernatural exploits that will compel the multitudes to Jesus on a daily basis.

10. **COMMUNION:** Father! Open my ears like Moses, call me by name like Elijah. I receive the anointing of fire and I move the glory clouds. I engage the prayer watches for total transfiguration in Jesus' name.

Give thanks for answered prayers!

INSTRUCTION:

1. At the midnight watch pray and sing scriptures. Locate God's word for at least 7 items and praise Him for double perfection and rest.

2. For debt cancellation: Sow a sacrificial seed (you can't buy a miracle but you can provoke heaven with your seed – 1 Kings 3:3).

DAY 15

WHITE AS LIGHT

Today is the fifteenth day of the fast and we will be looking at the truest and purest form of holiness. The brightest form of light that you could ever imagine was revealed on that mountain about our Lord Jesus Christ because He is the Light that lights every man that comes into the world **John 1:9**. The Bible tells us about this Refiner and Purifier - I love how the NLT renders **Malachi 3:2-3**,

> *"But who will be able to endure it when he comes? Who will be able to stand and face him when he appears? For he will be like a blazing fire that refines metal, or like a strong soap that bleaches clothes. He will sit like a refiner of silver, burning away the dross. He will purify the Levites, refining them like gold and silver, so that they may once again offer acceptable sacrifices to the Lord.*

Who are the Levites? These are the priests of the Most High God, set apart to serve the Lord exclusively in the Old Testament. Now the Lord has also made us kings and priests unto our God in Christ Jesus, we are set apart to worship the Lord in spirit and in truth. As you continue on this Mountain of Transfiguration, you will be transformed into the image of

Christ according to **2 Corinthians 3:18,**

> *But we all, with unveiled face, beholding as in a mirror the glory of the Lord, are being transformed into the same image from glory to glory, just as by the Spirit of the Lord.*

As you pay close attention to the word of God and follow the instructions released by the Spirit of the Lord on this mountain, you will be transformed into His image. No devil will be able to look you in the face and you will no longer struggle with the works of the flesh from today in Jesus' name.

Just as the butterfly transforms in stages and eventually emerges in full color and beauty, you will also emerge in full glory after the image of Christ. At first the butterfly is an egg that hatches into a caterpillar. As a caterpillar, it is very limited in movement and remains crawling on the ground like all other bugs. It may look very unattractive for a while and may even be mistaken for other insects like the centipede or millipede who will never get to fly. But this interesting bug-like creature or ground-kissing caterpillar then decides one day to shuts itself up in a cocoon or what is known as a chrysalis. In that state of separation, it hibernates and grows tremendously transforming over a period of time. The changes may not be noticed by outsiders but it is going through a process of metamorphosis and then suddenly, one day, without any warning a colorful creature of great beauty emerges out of the film that used to house it. That process of metamorphosis that happens to the butterfly is very similar to what happens to a believer when you fast and pray according to scriptures. You will no longer be the same again. Like Moses who went on the mountain of God and was transformed into a fearless enigma because he separated himself unto God. He was incubated in the chrysalis of God's presence and was supernaturally enabled to live a holy life that challenged his peers. He came out of the secret place glowing as white as light.

The same happened with the man Elijah, he was a man who lived as a beacon of light in his generation; when everyone else was living a timid life of compromise, he stood out for holiness and for the Holy One of Israel. So also will you stand out in your nation and generation as you are transformed into the image of the Lord on this mountain. You will emerge as white as light like our Lord Jesus Christ whose face shone and his robe glistened with flashing lights. You will be supernaturally empowered to live by the same grace. Sin will no longer have dominion over you as the Bible says in **Romans 6:14** because you are not under the law but under grace. You will learn to put off the old man with mastery and put on the new man which is created after God in righteousness and true holiness. You will become an expert at defeating the flesh and its carnal nature according to **Colossians 3:8-10**, *But now you yourselves are to put off all these: anger, wrath, malice, blasphemy, filthy language out of your mouth. Do not lie to one another, since you have put off the old man with his deeds, and have put on the new man who is renewed in knowledge according to the image of Him who created him, the Refiner's fire and the Fullers soap will cleanse and renew you for His service.*

We have established previously that we are power stations; we are the **transformers** of our generation. You and I are like the metal conduits used for conducting electrical energy but the power we conduct is that of the Omnipotent God to our generation. We all know that metals are good conductors of electricity and it is also common knowledge that the purer the metal, the better it conducts the power from the source. So also does the Lord refine us His fire and the water of His word purifies us. Malachi 3 says He will be like a blazing fire that refines metal, or like a strong soap that bleaches clothes. He will sit like a refiner of silver, burning away the dross. He burns off every worthless rubbish, trash and chaff in our lives. The Bible makes it clear that righteousness exalts a nation but sin is a reproach to any people; I pray that those little foxes that spoil the vine in your life will be thoroughly dealt with as you continue on this Mountain of Transfiguration in Jesus' name. Believe me, righteousness exalts! It is time for you to get that long awaited promotion in your career but it will only come by walking in righteousness. The Bible says he who does righteousness is righteous! No matter how you try in the flesh to be righteous, it is all like filthy rags. But you must learn to put the grace of Christ to work in order to live an empowered life over sin, this will yield the tangible fruits of righteousness that will become evident as you grow in His presence. Remember, you are a metal conductor - the more dross, the less power you carry or transmit but the purer the metal, the greater the power it transmits.

As a Transformer you are a change agent in your community and a power center to your world – you cannot blend in with the crowd. You are no longer permitted to tell the corporate lies at work. You can no longer cooperate with any cheating classmates during examinations. You are children of light and cannot afford to be a casualty carrying raw power and messing with filth. Remember this fire consumes evil but enhances good. When this fire touches a bad tree, it burns it to ashes but when it touches a good tree like the burning bush in Exodus 3, it enhances the glow – it burns but does not consume. You are no longer permitted to live by a double standard.

You are God's lamp-stand; you are on display for the world to see. You were set up as a lamp stand to give light in your community, school or work place. Lamps display glory and beauty.

Matthew 5:14-16,

> *"You are the light of the world. A city that is set on a hill cannot be hidden. Nor do they light a lamp and put it under a basket, but on a lampstand, and it gives light to all who are in the house. Let your light so shine before men, that they may see your good works and glorify your Father in heaven.*

Many Christians want to shine exclusively for Jesus but they are still full of dross – dead works of the flesh. They want God to promote them and display them but no one displays a tainted item. Most businesses only put their best item on the display window. You are heaven's best and must bring glory to the Father. You cannot afford to wear the marks of darkness anymore; you must shine as light. You can no longer carry around what the Bible calls the weight and sin that easily besets us. The weights weigh you down! Don't you get it? If you want to catch the eagle's flight and fly really high in destiny, then all the dead weights have got to go. You must shed both physical and carnal weights to gain spiritual muscle. You must be willing to stand out when others blend in. You must be willing to stick for the truth even when it cost you popularity among your peers. You can no longer be politically correct.

Many of us are more willing to please our peers instead of pleasing the Lord. We want God's exclusive treatment as someone special but treat Him as insignificant among our friends. We esteem popular opinion over scriptural opinion. He said, those who honor me, I will honor and those who despise me, I will lightly esteem. You must honor Him daily in the way you walk, talk and conduct yourself. If you are going to truly carry God's power and transmit it to the world, it is time to live a life of holiness – a life where no compromise is permitted, a life where the first person you talk to in the morning is Christ and the last person you converse with is the Holy Spirit. It is time to live by His words and not according to worldly trends. It is time to clean out the closet full of what **Ephesians 5:12** calls shameful...

> *For it is shameful even to speak of those things which are done by them in secret. But all things that are exposed are made manifest by the light.*

It is time to shine the light of the word of God on those dark and grey areas!

Without holiness, no man shall see God! Whether in a vision or face-to-face, whether on this side of eternity or the other side. The Bible says to take off the old man like a garment and put on the new man in **Ephesians 4:22-24** that you put off, concerning your former conduct, the old man which grows corrupt according to the deceitful lusts, and be renewed in the spirit of your mind, and that you put on the new man which was created according to God, in true righteousness and holiness. It is time for you true nature, your God nature to shine through like Jesus. His physical body dissolved in that instant of transfiguration and the real spirit shone through. You are not flesh; you are spirit! Moses saw God's glory while he lived on the earth, in fact God spoke about him in Numbers 12 that He talks with him face to face. You cannot see or hear God when you are toying with sin. You know why? God's holiness is blinding and consuming.

Hebrews 12:29,
> *For our God is a consuming fire.*

Fasting kills the flesh, it mortifies the flesh completely and destroys its carnal desires. When you abstain from food and feed on the word of God, you are empowering your spirit man to shine forth.

Don't fall for the traps of lies, anger or bitterness during this fast; they are unnecessary weights that will hinder you. You will see that as you leave all the weight behind, you will gain speed in your race of destiny and like Jesus you will emerge with dazzling robes as white as light! Receive grace to shine as light in Jesus' name! Exaltation is here for you! The Lord is the Refining Fire and the Fullers' soap - He alone can make your clothes become dazzling white, far whiter than any earthly bleach could ever make them. Acquaint yourself with Him today, receive instruction from His mouth and your life will never be the same again. It is time to stop living below your true potentials and start living fully according to His divine mandate for your life here on earth.
Catch fire in His presence and let the world watch you burn for His glory!!

It is time to pray!

DAY 15 PRAYER POINTS

1. Thank You Lord for this beautiful day of Holy Convocation unto you. Thank You for bringing me out of darkness to bring me into your kingdom of marvelous light.

2. Thank You for the grace to continue on this 21 days journey on the Mountain of Transfiguration. Thank You for supernatural life and joy unspeakable in your presence.

3. Thank You Lord for my family, friends and loved ones. Thank You for the assignment ahead of me and the grace to finish strong in Christ Jesus.

4. Father Lord, I shed all the weight and sin that easily beset me and move from the outer courts into the inner sanctuary of your presence. I am sanctified and meet for the Master's use in Jesus' name.

5. I receive the baptism of fire that makes me an effective channel of blessings to my generation. I burn every chaff and dross by your holy fire in Jesus' name. As the light of the world, I glow, I shine and I dazzle with God's glory.

6. Every works of the flesh that has limited the flow of the miraculous in my life from today catch fire and burn to ashes. Mention the areas you need to renounce before the Lord _____ (lying, anger, malice, bitterness, exaggerations, masturbation, fornication, witchcraft and sorcery e.g. consulting with a psychic or medium, stealing, pornography and the likes)

7. Righteousness exalts a nation but sin is a reproach to any people; therefore I denounce and disgrace every reproach that sin has brought into my life by the blood of Jesus! I am elevated for destiny; I enjoy promotion at work, at school and in my calling in Jesus' name. MY EXALTATION HAS COME!

8. Father Lord, purify me as silver and let me come out purer than gold. Make me a conductor of your power and let me display your light in the darkness of this world. I contact the power to heal the sick and set the captives free in Jesus' name.

9. As I continue on this mountain let my true nature emerge; let Your light shine in me and Your fire burn through me such that the sin nature is completely destroyed - I refuse to struggle with the flesh from today. I HAVE DOMINION!

10. **COMMUNION**: From this table I contact the Christ nature. God of Elijah, purge me by Your fire! God of Moses, show me Your glory. Father, transform me into Your image and Your glory in Jesus' name.

Give thanks for answered prayers!

INSTRUCTION: Write a list of the areas where you need to deal with the sin nature. Ask the CONSUMING FIRE to burn them to chaff as you go through them one by one (Use the 12 midnight or 3am watch).

DAY 16

ALONE WITH GOD

Our topic for today is ALONE WITH GOD. All the patriarchs of old who sought God's presence alone shook their generation mightily. Are you willing to seek the Lord with all your heart today? Are you ready to focus on Him alone about your life? Are you able to set the time aside to address that longstanding issue that has been making a mockery of your calling and destiny? Are you willing to cut off all the distractions and seek Him in a season of solitude – fasting, praying, praising and meditating exclusively on His word? If you are willing to pay the price, then get ready for a supernatural encounter with the King of Kings!

What does it mean to be alone with the Lord? It is the ability to cut out all the noise and get into that secret place of the Most High. **Psalm 91** says He who dwells in the secret place of the Most High shall abide under the shadow of the Almighty. The person who knows how to run into the Secret Place enjoys angelic protection and gains mastery over the forces of darkness. He is exempted from all the sicknesses that molest people out there and kept from any sudden destruction. His entire household enjoys divine covering because He has set

His heart to seek the Lord at all times. You will notice that when a man knows how to get alone with God and enter into the crook of the Lord's arm, he won't need to fight any battle on his own but the Man of War will take over all his battles. He will emerge from there a terror to the devil and a commander of circumstances. He will gain supernatural strength and operate with unusual stamina like Moses and Elijah.

He knows how to take advantage of the prayer watches when others are sleeping. He has learnt to shut out the noisy distractions from soap operas and discipline himself away from the addiction of social media. He has gained mastery over aimless internet browsing and now knows how to streamline unnecessary discussions with professional time-wasters on the phone. He is extremely focused while praying and studying the word of God. He has also mastered the act of walking away from the crowd to pray like Jesus did throughout His earthly ministry. Spending time in communion with the Father allowed Him to know exactly who He was and the details of His purpose and timing.

Luke 9:18,
> *And it happened, as He was alone praying, that His disciples joined Him, and He asked them, saying, "Who do the crowds say that I am?"*

He knew who He was - but did they? If you don't know what your assignment here on earth is all about, it is time to get alone with God!

We can see that Jesus was practically alone by Himself on the Mountain of Transfiguration praying – because the disciples had all dozed off.

My prayer is that you will come out of this mountain a champion to your world and a terror to the kingdom of darkness. Those things that once challenged you will be challenged by your authority in Jesus' name. So many people throw in the towel and give up when the battle gets intense. No!! When the battle gets intense is when you must intensify your prayer! When you are faced with that humiliating circumstance is the actual time to humble yourself under the mighty hand of God in prayer and fasting. Many don't know what it means to humble oneself.

James 4:10,

> *Humble yourselves in the sight of the Lord, and He will lift you up.*

In a couple of verses before that (**James 4:8**), the Bible says,

> *Draw near to God and He will draw near to you. Cleanse your hands, you sinners; and purify your hearts, you double-minded.*

When you are in the midst of spiritual warfare is not the time to dilly-dally between two opinions but the time to engage the secret tool of fasting and prayer. Just like what happened in **Ezra 8:21&23,**

> *Then I proclaimed a fast there at the river of Ahava, that we might humble ourselves before our God, to seek from Him the right way for us and our little ones and all our possessions. So we fasted and entreated our God for this, and He answered our prayer.*

Whenever you are faced with the dark battles of life that is when you go before the One who has never lost a battle before! Whenever you are experiencing what the Bible calls "exceeding sorrow", that is when you crawl into the secret place under the Shadow of the Almighty: Jesus showed us an example in

Matthew 26:36-41,

> *Then Jesus came with them to a place called Gethsemane, and said to the disciples, "Sit here while I go and pray over there." And He took with Him Peter and the two sons of Zebedee (James and John) and He began to be sorrowful and deeply distressed. Then He said to them, "My soul is exceedingly sorrowful, even to death. Stay here and watch with Me." (Watch with me means pray with me) He went a little farther and fell on His face, (HE PROSTRATED BEFORE THE FATHER) and prayed, saying, "O My Father, if it is possible, let this cup pass from Me; nevertheless, not as I will, but as You will."*

He prayed himself into the Father's will and when he was done, as usual, his buddies were sleeping. Those who should be His fellow intercessors were snoozing. Have you been stranded in a hole before? And you are looking for someone to pray with you but found none – put your mind to rest, our Lord has experienced the same. See verse 40-41,

> *Then He came to the disciples and found them sleeping, and said to Peter, "What! Could you not watch with Me one hour? Watch and pray, lest you enter into temptation. The spirit indeed is willing, but the flesh is weak."*

Many singles are struggling with the details and timing of their marital destiny. Like Ruth, you may need to seek the Lord at the midnight hour - the Bible records that she got up at midnight prostrating at the feet of a man called Boaz. I strongly advice that you prostrate at the Lord's feet not at any man's feet because I'm not so sure you can pull off what Ruth did without being ridiculed or taken advantage of.

Ruth 3:8-9,
> *Now it happened at midnight that the man was startled, and turned himself; and there, a woman was lying at his feet. And he said, "Who are you?" So she answered, "I am Ruth, your maidservant. Take your maidservant under your wing, for you are a close relative."*

Please singles, do not go to anyone at midnight; it may get you into a lot of trouble. But you can take advantage of the midnight watch going before your Maker in prayer to settle your case before him and like Ruth's case was settled in 24 hours; you also will get a speedy turnaround in Jesus mighty name.

Have you experienced any heartache in the past or sorrow to the point where you feel your heart might explode? Go to your Comforter in prayer; only He can comfort you like no one else. That was exactly what Jesus did and the Bible records that angels came to minister to Him after He prayed. Another woman we know who left everyone else to be alone with her God when she became very sorrowful was Hannah in **1 Samuel 1:12-13 & 17,**
> *And it happened, as she continued praying before the Lord, that Eli watched her mouth. Now Hannah spoke in her heart; only her lips moved, but her voice was not heard. Therefore Eli thought she was drunk. But she assured him she was just pouring out her soul before her Maker…Then Eli answered and said, "Go in peace, and the God of Israel grant your petition which you have asked of Him."*

She got her Samuel! You can pray your way into that miracle. There is a place you get to in prayer that you will look drunk to an onlooker. Many of us need to get there.

Get into that stubborn mode like Jacob that said, "I will not let you go until you bless me." This is one time you are allowed to be stubborn. He was alone with God to settle matters concerning his destiny!

Genesis 32:24,

Then Jacob was left alone; and a Man wrestled with him until the breaking of day. After he wrestled that night, he got his breakthrough by the morning light.

In the next chapter, we see how the Lord overturned an adverse situation in his favor.

Genesis 33:1-4,

Now Jacob lifted his eyes and looked, and there, Esau (his sworn enemy) was coming, and with him were four hundred men (an army). So he divided the children among Leah, Rachel, and the two maidservants. And he put the maidservants and their children in front, Leah and her children behind, and Rachel and Joseph last. Then he crossed over before them and bowed himself to the ground seven times, until he came near to his brother. But Esau ran to meet him, and embraced him, and fell on his neck and kissed him, and they wept (emphasis mine).

He also did something quite unusual when he saw that his nemesis was about to catch up with him - HE PROSTRATED BEFORE THE LORD seven times but his enemy's heart melted towards him. When he prostrated before the Lord, the Lord God turned the heart of his adversary in a heartbeat. Try Him now. He can reverse the irreversible!

During this fast, you must learn to cut off the excessive eating and drinking so you don't end up like the disciples who could not deal with that demon in the boy. They were known to love food and sleep.

Luke 5:34-35,

> *And He said to them, "Can you make the friends of the bridegroom fast while the bridegroom is with them? But the days will come when the bridegroom will be taken away from them; then they will fast in those days."*

When the disciples learned the secret of fasting and praying, they too became walking wonders on the earth. They put the grace of the Lord to work by walking in the Spirit and allowing the Holy Spirit to empower them into a life of supernatural exploits. Grace is for empowerment – the divine enablement to do what we could not do before with our human effort. Grace is not to be taken for granted but used to accomplish great exploits. Receive the grace to do what you could not do before now. Receive the grace to fast, pray and study the word like never before. Receive the grace to walk as Christ walked on the earth.

When you know how to be alone with God, you will enjoy preferential treatment and divine exemptions. God will grant you diplomatic access when others are shut out because your voice is recognized in heaven.

Exodus 24:9-10,

> *Then Moses went up, also Aaron, Nadab, and Abihu, and seventy of the elders of Israel, and they saw the God of Israel. And there was under His feet as it were a paved work of sapphire stone, and it was like the very heavens in its clarity. They all caught a glimpse of heaven but it was only Moses that went up into God's presence.*

We see that in verse 12 the Lord said to Moses,

> *"Come up to Me on the mountain and be there; and I will give you tablets of stone, and the law and commandments which I have written, that you may teach them."*

Did you know that Moses wrote **Psalm 91**? He caught the secret of the Lord's presence. He knew what it meant to be in the secret place. The places where no one else dared enter was the very place Moses walked into without fear. Exodus 24:16-18,

> *Now the glory of the Lord rested on Mount Sinai, and the cloud covered it six days. And on the seventh day He called to Moses out of the midst of the cloud. The sight of the glory of the Lord was like a consuming fire on the top of the mountain in the eyes of the children of Israel. So Moses went into the midst of the cloud and went up into the mountain. And Moses was on the mountain forty days and forty nights.*

We see that the other patriarch on the Mountain of Transfiguration (Elijah) also knew how to run into the secret place of the Most High. He went to be alone with God when the forces of witchcraft threatened his life in **1 Kings 19:9-13**,

> *And there he went into a cave, and spent the night in that place; and behold, the word of the Lord came to him, and He said to him, "What are you doing here, Elijah?" So he said, "I have been very zealous for the Lord God of hosts; for the children of Israel have forsaken Your covenant, torn down Your altars, and killed Your prophets with the sword. I alone am left; and they seek to take my life."*

At first he was lamenting and whining to the Lord like most of us do when we become frustrated with our assignment or we think that we have come to the end of the road. The Lord set Elijah straight with stern correction and when he obeyed and followed through, the Lord answered him with specific instructions and details for not only his own assignment but that of the succeeding generation of leaders.

> *Then He said, "Go out, and stand on the mountain before the Lord." And behold, the Lord passed by, and a great and strong wind tore into the mountains and broke the rocks in pieces before the Lord, but the Lord was not in the wind; and after the wind an earthquake, but the Lord was not in the earthquake; and after the earthquake a fire, but the Lord was not in the fire; and after the fire a still small voice. So it was, when Elijah heard it, that he wrapped his face in his mantle and went out and stood in the entrance of the cave. Suddenly a voice came to him, and said, "What are you doing here, Elijah?"*

GOD SHOWED UP!

It is time you shut out the noise and learn to praise the Lord like the man David who knew how to seek the Lord in solitude. He was a shepherd boy who became accustomed to taking lonely walks with the Lord while watching his father's flock. He was empowered to become the shepherd of God's people who eventually cut off principalities called Goliath in **1 Samuel 17:43-45**,

> *So the Philistine said to David, "Am I a dog, that you come to me with sticks?" And the Philistine cursed David by his gods. And the Philistine said to David, "Come to me, and I will give your flesh to the birds of the air and the beasts of the field!" Then David said to the Philistine, "You come to me with a sword, with a spear, and with a javelin. But I come to you in the name of the Lord of hosts, the God of the armies of Israel, whom you have defied.*

Those days alone in the field, he had mastered how fight the adversary hiding under the shadow of God's presence. One of the names of Jehovah that I love most is the one David used to defeat Goliath – He is the LORD OF HOST: He controls both the angelic and satanic host. He commands warrior angels and He can use anyone of them to fight your battle. He is the Captain of the Host. The Captain of the Armies of Israel; The Captain of the Angelic Army! The Master and Commander of the universe.

He will fight all those invisible battles on your behalf. He will defeat those cowardly strangers that only show up in your dreams at night. He is Spirit and He can show up anywhere in the universe to fight a battle because He created the entire universe. The sky is the train of His garment and the stars are the ornaments on His glorious robe. He fills all in all. No demon can escape Him! Invite Him into that impossible battle and make Him your Defender!

It is time to pray.

DAY 16 PRAYER POINTS

1. Thank You Lord for this wonderful time in your presence. Thank You Lord for showing me the power of the Secret Place.

2. Thank You Lord for transforming my mind and renewing my spirit on this Mountain of Transfiguration. Thank You for the daily dosage of empowering revelations.

3. Thank You Lord for the changes I am experiencing in my body, soul and spirit. Thank You for increasing my strength like the eagle on this mountain.

4. LORD OF HOST! Show all my enemies that you are my DEFENDER! Defeat every household wickedness from my father's house, my mother's house and from my in-laws' house. Contend with my contender and harass my harasser in Jesus' name!

5. As I seek you alone this season, let me find you. Let me gain access to your secret place like Moses. Speak to me like Elijah and call me by name like your Son Jesus Christ; give me the specific instructions for my destiny!

6. From this Mountain of Transfiguration, let me emerge as a giant killer and anoint me with the fire that terrorizes the kingdom of darkness. Grant me mastery over the flesh so I can breakthrough in the spirit in Jesus' name.

7. Lord like Moses let me hear your voice and like Elijah open my inner ears. As I separate myself in solitude, let me experience the invisible and let me access the inaudible. FATHER, CALL ME OUT BY NAME!

8. I distract every distraction and I frustrate every frustration in Jesus' name. I come against every scourging of the tongue and I silence every strange noise attacking my prayer altar – they are disgraced and condemned according to the word of the Lord!

9. I declare that every blessing with my name tag on it this year is released to me by fire as I seek the Lord in prayer and fasting. I take back all that is mine in Jesus' name – Jabez got his enlargement, Hannah got the fruit of the womb, Jacob got his destiny settled and Moses got divine access. I take back my _____ (mention what was stolen before the Lord) marriage, children, immigration papers, job, promotion etc.

10. COMMUNION: From this communion table, I tap into the grace of Christ to pray through the prayer watches and persevere through the night watches. I gain mastery in the place of prayer and fasting to emerge a transformer to my generation.

Give thanks for answered prayers!

INSTRUCTION: Go before the Lord at midnight with your list of seven items prostrating before Him. Settle those matters that make you shed secret tears; the LORD OF HOST will arise.

DAY 17

SUPER-HUMAN STRENGTH

Today is the seventeenth day and the number seventeen reveals the difference between the Old and New Covenant according to **Hebrews 12:18-24**: For you have not come to the mountain that may be touched (1) and that burned with fire (2) and to blackness (3) and darkness (4) and tempest (5) and the sound of a trumpet (6) and the voice of words (7) And so terrifying was the sight that Moses said, "I am exceedingly afraid and trembling." This first was Mount Sinai.

Verse 22 now says, "But you have come to Mount Zion (1) and to the city of the living God (2) the heavenly Jerusalem (3) to an innumerable company of angels (4) to the general assembly (5) and church of the firstborn who are registered in heaven (6) to God the Judge of all (7) to the spirits of just men made perfect (8) to Jesus the Mediator of the new covenant (9) and to the blood of sprinkling that speaks better things than that of Abel (10). HALLELUJAH!

What stands out to me the most of all the seventeen is the **Mediator** of the New Covenant and the **blood** of sprinkling that speaks better things than the blood of Abel. What does the blood of Abel speak of? It speaks of vengeance and no mercy at all. The blood of Jesus was shed in the same way as Abel's but it speaks from the ground MERCY for us and not VENGEANCE. On this seventeenth day, we will be looking into the blood that speaks. This is the blood that transforms us from human to superhuman. How do we access this blood? First of all, through the miracle of salvation. It is through our Lord Jesus the Mediator of the New Covenant.

Secondly, it is administered to us through the communion table on a daily basis. Paul teaching in **1 Corinthians 11:26** said as often as you partake of the communion you proclaim the Lord's death till He comes. That means you are speaking into effect everything that Christ died for on the Cross of Calvary.

This table is presented to us with a meal that consists of the flesh and the blood of Jesus. The Apostle Paul calls this the Cup of Blessing in **1 Corinthians 10:16**,

> *The cup of blessing which we bless, is it not the communion of the blood of Christ? The bread which we break, is it not the communion of the body of Christ?*

It is very crucial for every believer to partake of the communion on a regular basis and not once a month or ceremonially as we have been made to believe. The disciples broke bread from house to house daily in **Act 2:46** and all that Christ represented was present in their lives. You can see that all the miracles Christ did in Matthew chapter 9 was replicated in **Acts 9** by the disciples as well – paralysis cured, blind eye restored and dead raised back to life. We all know that they did not joke about the Communion Table from the first day the Lord Jesus instructed them to eat it. The more you eat the flesh and drink His blood, the more like Jesus you become.

I want to quickly point out that when Jesus was transfigured before the disciples on the Mountain of Transfiguration, His superhuman nature was revealed to them in **Matthew 17:2-3**, His face shone like the sun, and His clothes became as white as the light. And behold, Moses and Elijah appeared to them, talking with Him. If you look through the scriptures you will see that these two men also ate bread from heaven and they both displayed unusual strength. They lived a supernatural life and operated as super-humans. Elijah ate this bread in **1 Kings 19:8**,

> *So he arose, and ate and drank; and he went in the strength of that food forty days and forty nights as far as Horeb, the mountain of God.*

In his lifetime, he raised the dead and outran king's chariots. He was known to appear and disappear at will. He operated in the miraculous and compelled rain and fire on the enemy on a regular basis. He literally walked and lived a supernatural life.

The same happened with the man Moses – the entire nation ate Manna in **Psalm 78:24-25**, *The Lord had rained down manna on them to eat, And given them of the bread of heaven. Men ate angels' food; He sent them food to the full.* The Bible records that Moses' natural strength was not abated. At 120 years, he was still super strong.

Deuteronomy 34:7,
> *Moses was one hundred and twenty years old when he died. His eyes were not dim nor his natural vigor diminished.*

Both his physical and spiritual vision did not grow dim. Is it possible for the eye to see the one who made and go blind? It has no choice but to see clearly! Moses heard and wrote down the word of God whenever he was on the mountain fasting.

He was eating spiritual food that extended his physical lifespan beyond his contemporaries. He saw farther and heard God clearer than many patriarchs of old. His body refused to die even when his time was up.

DID YOU KNOW THAT JESUS ALSO HAD A SPECIAL BODY?

The writer of Hebrew was speaking concerning Jesus in the 10th chapter and the 5th verse:

> *Therefore, when He came into the world, He said: "Sacrifice and offering You did not desire, but a body You have prepared for Me.*

This body was not tainted and could not be weakened by sin. You will see that He also appeared and disappeared at will when His time was not yet up and the Pharisees tried to arrest Him. In due time, He bore the punishment of our sins and the quickening spirit that raised Him from the dead was indwelling Him all the time. His life was not taken from Him, He laid down His life. You can get that same body from this table; a body of super strength and quickening spirit! He said in John 6:48, *I am the bread of life* and in **John 6:51**, *I am the living bread which came down from heaven. If anyone eats of this bread, he will live forever; and the bread that I shall give is My flesh, which I shall give for the life of the world.*

You need to eat of this flesh and drink of His blood to enjoy this divine nature. His blood will infuse you with supernatural life and make you superhuman. You will exchange mortality for immortality; you will switch that which is weak and sick for that which can never get sick nor die.

Did you ever hear of Elijah being sick? Or Moses or even our Lord Jesus Christ? He continues in **John 6:53-58** -

> *Then Jesus said to them, "Most assuredly, I say to you, unless you eat the flesh of the Son of Man and drink His blood, you have no life in you. Whoever eats My flesh and drinks My blood has eternal life, and I will raise him up at the last day. For My flesh is food indeed, and My blood is drink indeed. He who eats My flesh and drinks My blood abides in Me, and I in him. As the living Father sent Me, and I live because of the Father, so he who feeds on Me will live because of Me. This is the bread which came down from heaven—not as your fathers ate the manna, and are dead. He who eats this bread will live forever."*

This table gives life! He taught His disciples how to tap into this life in **Luke 22:19-20,**

> *And He took bread, gave thanks and broke it, and gave it to them, saying, "This is My body which is given for you; do this in remembrance of Me."*

Likewise, He also took the cup after supper, saying,

> *"This cup is the new covenant in My blood, which is shed for you.*

Now talking of the blood that speaks – Like I mentioned earlier, Paul by revelation wrote the same in **1 Corinthians 11:23-26,**

> *For I received from the Lord that which I also delivered to you: that the Lord Jesus on the same night in which He was betrayed took bread; and when He had given thanks, He broke it and said, "Take, eat; this is My body which is broken for you; do this in remembrance of Me." In the same manner He also took the cup after supper, saying, "This cup is the new covenant in*

My blood. This do, as often as you drink it, in remembrance of Me." For as often as you eat this bread and drink this cup, you proclaim the Lord's death till He comes.

I LOVE THE LAST PART THAT SAYS - you proclaim the Lord's death till He comes. What does the Lord's death represent and what does it proclaim? It proclaims freedom from poverty and slavery; it proclaims divine healing, victory over death and all principalities and power. His blood puts you in His class.

The type of the Communion Table was instituted in the Old Testament and it had the same effect. Taking vengeance for the children of Israel and setting them free from centuries of bondage in slavery.

Psalm 105:36-37, 40

He also destroyed all the firstborn in their land, the first of all their strength. He also brought them out with silver and gold, And there was none feeble among His tribes. The people asked, and He brought quail, And satisfied them with the bread of heaven. He fed them to satisfaction and They were not sick. From this mountain of the Lord, where the blood speaks you will no longer experience sickness.

By this table, you are set free from generational poverty and whenever the death angels see the blood, they pass over you. When you take the Communion, you are enforcing all that Christ died for on the Cross including longevity. Some may be wondering what the Communion have to do with fasting and prayer? What role has the Communion got to play in winning all the dark battles arrayed against me? Let us take a quick look at a type of the Communion Table displayed under the Old Testament in **Exodus 12**.

We will only look at specific verses but please go back and read through the entire chapter diligently in your own time.

Exodus12: THE PASSOVER

Verses 5-8,

Your lamb shall be without blemish, a male of the first year. You may take it from the sheep or from the goats. Now you shall keep it until the fourteenth day of the same month. Then the whole assembly of the congregation of Israel shall kill it at twilight. And they shall take some of the blood and put it on the two doorposts and on the lintel of the houses where they eat it. Then they shall eat the flesh on that night; roasted in fire, with unleavened bread and with bitter herbs they shall eat it.

IMPLICATION: Jesus is the Lamb of God without any blemish.

Verses 11-14,

And thus you shall eat it: with a belt on your waist, your sandals on your feet, and your staff in your hand. So you shall eat it in haste. It is the Lord's Passover. 'For I will pass through the land of Egypt on that night, and will strike all the firstborn in the land of Egypt, both man and beast; and against all the gods of Egypt I will execute judgment: I am the Lord. Now the blood shall be a sign for you on the houses where you are. And when I see the blood, I will pass over you; and the plague shall not be on you to destroy you when I strike the land of Egypt. 'So this day shall be to you a memorial; and you shall keep it as a feast to the Lord throughout your generations. You shall keep it as a feast by an everlasting ordinance.

IMPLICATION: It moves God swiftly into action on our behalf invoking vengeance upon all our enemies.

Verses 35-36,
> *Now the children of Israel had done according to the word of Moses, and they had asked from the Egyptians articles of silver, articles of gold, and clothing. And the Lord had given the people favor in the sight of the Egyptians, so that they granted them what they requested. Thus they plundered the Egyptians.*

IMPLICATION: We got the same order of favor in Christ Jesus who became poor so that we can be rich. We enjoy a divine exchange from poverty to riches.

I would like you to note that the strange battles that Moses had been fighting against the forces of Egypt before that time bowed out to the blood sacrifice. There is power in the blood! After the Lord's Passover; Pharaoh bowed out in defeat. First, all the firstborn died in every single household with one single blow of the Lord of Host. Next, the children of Israel were released suddenly from the bondage of the taskmaster, from hard labor and slavery. I declare that anyone experiencing any form of bondage physical, spiritual, emotional or psychological is set free in Jesus' mighty name. I declare that every stubborn enemy following you, will be given in exchange for you in the name of Jesus! You will also note that wherever the blood was seen, the angel of death passed over. You bear the marks of our Lord Jesus Christ in your body. Death cannot touch you and evil cannot slay any member of your family. Rather, the angels of death will work for you in this strange battle and defeat every force of darkness in your life because our God is the Lord of Hosts.

YOUR HEALTH IS ALSO COVERED!

The cup of blessing imparts eternal life and longevity. The Bible says they ate angels' food and none was feeble among them. This supernatural meal is just like an intravenous injection (I.V) that resuscitates the believer from within. It infuses wisdom and power to the consumer. The Bible makes us to understand that Jesus is the wisdom and the power of God in 1 Corinthians 1:24&30. So when you eat His flesh and drink His blood you become more like Him; you manifest His divine nature. YOU GET SUPER STRENGTH AND SUPER-BRAINS. Your strength is renewed (power) and your understanding becomes enlightened (wisdom) - It becomes flooded with light because remember; He is the Light that lights every man that comes into the world.

As a student you can tap into his wealth of wisdom and supernatural intelligence.

Also when he broke bread with the disciples, their eyes became open.

Luke 24:30-31,

> *Now it came to pass, as He sat at the table with them, that He took bread, blessed and broke it, and gave it to them. Then their eyes were opened and they knew Him; and He vanished from their sight.*

Not physical eyes but the eyes of their mind. The more you eat His flesh and drink His blood, the more light fills you up. When you eat the bread with understanding, it has the ability to release divine provision and disarm your enemies without sweat. Jesus said as often as you do it, you proclaim the Lord's death until He comes. What does the death of Christ represent? Vengeance on our enemies! He spoiled principalities and powers triumphing over them in victory! He broke every yoke of sicknesses and diseases!

He brought us out of darkness into His marvelous light! He redeemed us from the curse of the law! He wore the crown of thorns on his head or brain so our brain could resume super speed like Adam and even better than Adam. He became poor for us to become rich. He died young so we can live long. He shed his blood on the ground that was cursed so that we don't have to operate under the curse of sweating and toiling anymore. He died without offspring or a wife so you can enjoy marital bliss. He has the church as His bride and we are His offspring through salvation. He paid the price in full so we don't have to bear the shame and guilt of sin anymore. We are completely free! Free to live in dominion and fulfill His assignment for each of our lives and the church as a whole.

This Cup of Blessing also imparts enabling grace and uncommon strength to go on long fasts like our Lord Jesus. We can also pray through the watches just like He did. The table confers uncommon strength. I have mentioned many times that the first time I ever did an extended fast, by day ten, I was fainting but the Lord instructed me to start taking the Communion daily and I was supernaturally strengthened to finish strong! I have broken every fast with the Communion ever since. It makes you superhuman. You won't get sick or weak like others do. I really find it funny when someone comes out of a fast saying they are weak or sick – I know right away that they did not do it right. Fasting as prescribed in scriptures empowers us and does not make us weak.

You might be asking now, so how do I get this Communion? Do I need to buy it from a special store? No, not really! You just need a simple fruit juice some people use (non-alcoholic) wine to represent the blood and regular bread to represent the flesh. Most people prefer the unleavened bread or salt-less crackers. Any of them will be sufficient. From today, every time you fast please make sure you break with the Holy Communion and you will see the difference. The Bible says teach it to your children and observe it in your generations. As often as you do you are enforcing your victory over the power of the enemy wrought in Christ.

This table is for children (saved) not dogs (unsaved), it is okay for the dogs to eat the crumbs that fall off the table but it will have no lasting effect. It will just become an additional problem if the eater is unsaved. The Bible calls it eating in an unworthy manner. Please note that the flesh and blood can discriminate between children and dogs. It imparts life and super strength to the children but makes the dogs sick and causes them to sleep (sleep here means death) you can read **1 Corinthians 11:27-30**,

> *Therefore whoever eats this bread or drinks this cup of the Lord in an unworthy manner will be guilty of the body and blood of the Lord. But let a man examine himself, and so let him eat of the bread and drink of the cup. For he who eats and drinks in an unworthy manner eats and drinks judgment to himself, not discerning the Lord's body. For this reason many are weak and sick among you, and many sleep.*

Don't get into the religion of it. Like Apostle Paul said, eating it carelessly but do it with reverence and understanding according to scriptures. My prayer is that your health will spring forth speedily as you observe this ordinance. I have personally tried and tasted it. It works! I don't fall sick since I discovered this secret and my mind has become supernaturally enabled. I can safely say: my mind has become electrified! I am walking into the realm of the miraculous by this table today and I'm placing a demand on all it has to offer. Will you join me? I want to see open visions like Moses and hear Him call out my name like Elijah.

It is time to pray.

DAY 17 PRAYER POINTS

1. Thank You Lord for this day and the beautiful revelation imparted to me on this mountain. Thank You for transforming me daily by Your word.

2. Thank You Lord for the communion table and the uncommon strength that it infuses to me. Thank You for Your body broken for me and Your blood that was shed for the remission of my sins.

3. Thank You Lord for bringing me to Mount Zion and for the Blood of Sprinkling that speaks mercy for me but vengeance on my enemies.

4. Father Lord, let the blood of Jesus speak for me today against every generational battle. I plead the blood against inherited sickness, generational poverty, failure at the edge of success, household wickedness, sorcery and divination, witchcraft forces, prayerlessness and powerlessness, strange afflictions, ungodly delay, limitations and stagnation, barrenness, untimely death _____ (Make your own list).

5. From this table, I contact supernatural strength to pray and fast. I contact the ability to operate in the miraculous like Moses and Elijah. As I eat the flesh and drink the blood, I manifest my

Lord Jesus Christ to the world on a daily basis.

6. I am supernaturally empowered to run my race like Elijah. I am supernaturally enlightened to see into the spirit realm like Moses and I shine as the light of the world like my Master Jesus. I HAVE THE MIND OF CHRIST!

7. Christ is the wisdom and power of God; I operate His super-speed mind and I put on His super-strength as a garment. Sicknesses flees when they see me and demons tremble out of their hideouts when they hear my voice in Jesus' name.

8. Jesus became poor so that I can become rich; I am richly blessed in the work of my hands. I am blessed to be a channel of blessing and empowered to empower others – my time of favor has come! I defeat the strongman of borrowing and shatter the shackles of poverty by the blood of Jesus.

9. Like Moses, I am enabled to fast and like Elijah I will go in the strength of this table. I mount up with the wings of an eagle and I run the race of destiny tirelessly. My vision will not grow dim and as my strength will not diminish in Jesus' name. I HAVE SUPER-STRENGTH!

10. COMMUNION: From this table, make me like Jesus. Transform me into the image of Christ; fill me with His passion and compassion. Change me into a world changer! I exchange mortality for immortality and put off the natural for the supernatural life!!

Give thanks for answered prayers!

INSTRUCTION: At midnight the Lord struck all the firstborn of Egypt in Exodus 12:29. Get up at midnight to address that stubborn enemy or unrepentant adversary. Speak the BLOOD OF SPRINKLING over the matter(s). Administer the Communion.

DAY 18

WORLD CHANGERS

Today is the eighteenth day of this fast. In **Luke 18:1**, Jesus spoke a parable to them, saying that men always ought to pray and not lose heart. Since the first day of this fast, we have been talking about one form of prayer or the other. Do you know that heaven is counting on your prayer and intercession for the land where you live? Did you know that you could usher in a revival through your prayers? Did you know that you could change the entire world from that your little corner? God is looking for an intercessor, a man who will stand in the gap to pray His will to fruition and His Kingdom to manifestation on planet earth.

He is looking for those whose hearts are connected to His purpose to show himself mighty on their behalf. He is waiting for his people called by His name to pray according to **2 Chronicles 16:9**,

> *For the eyes of the Lord run to and fro throughout the whole earth, to show Himself strong on behalf of those whose heart is loyal to Him.*

In **2 Chronicles 7:14-16** He said,

> *If My people who are called by My name will humble themselves, and pray and seek My face, and turn from their wicked ways, then I will hear from heaven, and will forgive their sin and heal their land. Now My eyes will be open and My ears attentive to prayer made in this place. For now I have chosen and sanctified this house, that My name may be there forever; and My eyes and My heart will be there perpetually.*

God strategically planted you in that location, nation and this generation for a purpose. You are not in that location by accident. No matter how much you despise that place you live, you were pre-appointed by God to live there. See **Acts 17:26**,

> *And He has made from one blood every nation of men to dwell on all the face of the earth, and has determined their pre-appointed times and the boundaries of their dwellings.*

Like Esther, the Bible said that you were born for such a time as this but if you refuse to cooperate with God, He will find a replacement. You will not be replaced in the Kingdom agenda in Jesus' mighty name.

As we study the prayer life of Jesus and the two patriarchs who appeared on the Mountain of Transfiguration with Him, we see that they did not pray their own selfish agenda but it was mainly about Kingdom agenda. When Jesus taught the disciples to pray in **Matthew 6:9-13**, it was about the Lord's will being done on earth as it is done in heaven. He taught us to pray down God's kingdom on the earth – He said, "Thy kingdom come!" In **John 17:1-end**, we can see that He glorified the Father exceedingly in this passage of scripture; it was never about him at all but all about what the Father wanted.

He went ahead to intercede for His disciples and finally prayed for all believers in the world at large (even when He had not died and there was none of us yet). Today, everywhere you look, you can see the impact of the prayer of Jesus. He prayed intensely and fervently locally but His impact reaches the far ends of the world. You may look like a local intercessor but before God, you are not a local champion but a world champion. He honors the prayer of the watchmen – those who enforce His will on the earth day and night on their knees.

You can see that the same goes for Moses— he interceded for the entire nation of Israel when God was about to destroy them for their sin of idolatry. He was so unselfish in his intercession despite the offer the Lord made him – see **Exodus 32:10-14**,

> *Now therefore, let Me alone, that My wrath may burn hot against them and I may consume them. And I will make of you a great nation." Then Moses pleaded with the Lord his God, and said: "Lord, why does Your wrath burn hot against Your people whom You have brought out of the land of Egypt with great power and with a mighty hand? Why should the Egyptians speak, and say, 'He brought them out to harm them, to kill them in the mountains, and to consume them from the face of the earth'? Turn from Your fierce wrath, and relent from this harm to Your people. Remember Abraham, Isaac, and Israel, Your servants, to whom You swore by Your own self, and said to them, 'I will multiply your descendants as the stars of heaven; and all this land that I have spoken of I give to your descendants, and they shall inherit it forever.'" So the Lord relented from the harm which He said He would do to His people.*

HOW MANY WILL NOT JUMP AT THE OFFER TO BECOME GREAT WHILE GOD DESTROYED THE DISOBEDIENT?

It sounded good, right? But not Moses, He reasoned with God to please spare the nation and negotiated with Him for surpassing mercy. No wonder the Lord loved this guy! Many theologians say that Moses was really a shadow of everything Christ came to do for humanity. Time will not permit us to go through all the shadows of Christ on this day but the Passover meal in **Exodus 12** and the communion in **1 Corinthians 11:23** is one. The serpent lifted up to save the children of Israel in **Numbers 21:9** is another type of the Cross – Jesus said if I be lifted high, I will draw all men unto me. Another similarity between Jesus and Moses was the death sentence against all male children when Moses was born. The same sentence was given when Herod knew that Christ was born. Please search in your spare time and you will see many –shadows of Christ. The best is the difference between Mount Sinai and Mount Zion (that was mentioned in the previous lesson). Moses brought the law while Jesus brought grace. Let us also take a look at these at another time in a different lesson.

Moses interceded for the nation of Israel in **Exodus 17:11-13**,
And so it was, when Moses held up his hand, that Israel prevailed; and when he let down his hand, Amalek prevailed....

Whether you know it or not, your prayer positively impacts your nation and the lack of it may be the reason it is in disrepair. One thing I love about our Lord is that He never leaves an intercessor un-promoted. Many people want to have global influence but they do not know that it starts from being a local influence. When God is seeing a vision, it is never limited to a location but He is seeing the global view of that thing.

See the progression in **Acts 1:8**, *But you shall receive power when the Holy Spirit has come upon you; and you shall be witnesses to Me in Jerusalem, and in all Judea and Samaria, and to the end of the earth."*

Local influence → National influence → Global influence.

I remember many years ago the Lord showed me these levels of influence in prayer – starting at my college campus, then the youth fellowship of my church that had branches all over the nation and then He moved me to the ends of the earth. That is how God sees! You may start from local but He is taking you global. I have since been part of many groundbreaking work of starting new campus fellowships and youth ministries in the United States but it all started from my local city in Nigeria. He that is faithful in little is also faithful in much. Start where you are now, your promotion before the Lord depends on it.

We all know without saying that the man Elijah was a prayer machine who shook the nations and is still shaking the world in influence today. The Bible records concerning him in **James 5:17-18,**

> *Elijah was a man with a nature like ours, and he prayed earnestly that it would not rain; and it did not rain on the land for three years and six months. And he prayed again, and the heaven gave rain, and the earth produced its fruit.*

He prayed down God's fire and there was a purging – a revival in the land. He rebuilt the Lord's altar for the twelve tribes of Israel. He was feared by kings and powerful armies. He was a force to reckon with. He shook the kingdom of darkness and it was never about his own agenda but he was zealous for the Lord. There is no place where fervent prayer is being mentioned today, that you won't hear the name of Elijah –

people pray to the God of Elijah, who answers by fire!

God is looking for men like Elijah today. Women who will pray down His fire and exit on chariots of fire. Did you know Christ also went up in the clouds like Elijah did? He raised up the son of a widow just like Jesus did. He was also a type, a shadow of things to come. Go and study these men whom the Lord revealed with our Lord Jesus on the Mountain of Transfiguration, you will be amazed at what He can do with you as well. You must pray the will of God into that neighborhood like a vigilante – day and night till testimonies break forth. **Isaiah 62:6-7** says,

> *I have set watchmen on your walls, O Jerusalem; They shall never hold their peace day or night nor keep silent, And give Him no rest till He makes Jerusalem a praise in the earth.*

He planted you there for a purpose – see **Ezekiel 33:7**,

> *"So you, son of man: I have made you a watchman for the house of Israel; therefore you shall hear a word from My mouth and warn them for Me.*

God does not hold back His secret from intercessors; He shares intimate details of things with them before they ever happen. Amos 3:7 says that God does nothing except He informs his servant the prophet. We have established in previous teaching that prophets are made in the womb of prayer – they have learned to watch and wait on the tower of prayer. A prophet is not one in mouth alone, but someone who knows how to engage the prayer watches. Nothing must happen without you having inkling from the Lord, like His friend Abraham in **Genesis 18:17-23**,

> *And the Lord said, "Shall I hide from Abraham what I am doing, since Abraham shall surely become a great and mighty*

nation, and all the nations of the earth shall be blessed in him? God told him He was about to destroy Sodom, but Abraham still stood before the Lord interceding saying, "Would You also destroy the righteous with the wicked?

You must pray the government into God's will.

Isaiah 60:17b-18,

> "I will also make your officers peace, And your magistrates righteousness. Violence shall no longer be heard in your land, Neither wasting nor destruction within your borders; But you shall call your walls Salvation, And your gates Praise.

But you know what? Many of us feel we have outgrown our present location or nation. We want to move to a new house or a new state but we haven't completed our divine assignment in our current location. We want shortcuts but until you touch that life, save that soul or pray that city through you may be stuck there for a while. You must pray all those in your building into the kingdom, that block where you live, that city, that state, that nation and your generation. In order to set Kairos time in motion, start using you Kronos time well in prayer by observing the prayer watches not selfishly but praying for those people in your neighborhood that you don't even know by name. There is a tremendous blessing loaded in the land but you must first fulfill the intercessory part of the deal. Promotion awaits you as you pray for that local change and your prayer fire will ignite nations like Elijah.

God is calling you and I to join Him in the glorious mission of kingdom expansion. In **John 15:16** Jesus said,

> You did not choose Me, but I chose you and appointed you that you should go and bear fruit, and that your fruit should remain,

that whatever you ask the Father in My name He may give you.

Hallelujah! In that scripture lies a key to answered prayers. When you bear fruits that remain, you will have an open access in prayer; anything you ask will be done. God is very passionate about winning souls; the entire Bible is written about this – if you run with the father's highest priority, then you will get all your priorities met as well. He will ensure that you receive all your desires and this is confirmed in **Psalm 37:4,**

Delight yourself also in the Lord, And He shall give you the desires of your heart.

In the place of prayer, you can engage a concept called PRAYER-EVANGELISM?

Psalm 2:8,
Ask of Me, and I will give You the nations for Your inheritance, And the ends of the earth for Your possession.

It is winning souls through fervent and consistent prayers. If you are too timid to preach at least you can pray! Nothing happens by accident. That school you attend was orchestrated by God for you to touch lives. That job you got out of all the others who interviewed alongside with you was because God wants you to reach a soul for Him there (maybe the coworker who may never attend church in their lifetime). You're in that neighborhood because God planted you there to intercede for the people and take over the land for Him. Stop waiting for someone else to do it. You can pray them into the kingdom and ignite the world for Jesus.

Do you have a prayer list for your unsaved friends? Neighbors, bosses or co-workers? They already know there is something different about you and depending on your level of walk with the Lord, you may still be too timid to share the gospel with them but you can pray. You can intercede for them. In fact, your prayer has tremendous power because you will be able to disarm any strong man controlling their lives. **Matthew 12:29** says,

> *How can one enter a strong man's house and plunder his goods, unless he first binds the strong man? And then he will plunder his house.*

You might be wondering what this means - there is a controlling force out there that influences everyone who is not yet saved. 2 Thessalonians 2:7 talks about the mystery of (iniquity) that is already at work; your prayer can shatter that demonic influence. Your prayers can bring warrior angels on the scene like Moses, Elijah and Jesus.

Stop being so timid, you are the solution the whole world is crying for!

Romans 8:19,

> *For the earnest expectation of the creation eagerly waits for the manifestation or revealing of the sons of God.*

I dare say, the earnest expectation of creation eagerly waits for the manifestation of world changers! Take a power walk around your neighborhood praying in tongues. Wherever the sole of your feet steps God said it is given to you. Claim the souls for Jesus. Take the land for Him like the children of Israel walked round Jericho. Physical and spiritual walls of barrier will begin to crumble before you! You will then decree a thing and it will be established unto you! That is the key to answered prayers!!

It is time to pray.

DAY 18 PRAYER POINTS

1. Thank You Lord for today's revelation and instruction on the Mountain of Transfiguration. Thank You for showing me the secret of being an intercessor.

2. Thank You Lord for calling me out as Your watchman. Thank You for the privilege of sharing Your secrets and knowing things before they happen.

3. Thank You Lord for leading me through this season of fasting and prayer - changing me and renewing me by your Spirit in the inner man. Thank You for the gift of life.

4. Father Lord, open my eyes to see what You see about my city, nation and generation. Grant me insight into Your divine agenda for my generation in Jesus' name.

5. As a watchman, help me to engage the prayer watches for my location, nation and generation. I receive the grace to pray for my nation and leaders so that godly wisdom will influence the laws of the land.

6. Lord, I pray for my city (name it), nation (name it) and generation. Lord, restore the splendor of my nation for we have become a dwarf among the nations. Restore the excellence of my people. Waste all the wasters and destroy all the emptiers in Jesus' name.

He who scatters has come up before your face. He who scatters has come up before your face. Man the fort! Watch the road! Strengthen your flanks! Fortify your power mightily. For the Lord will restore the excellence of Jacob Like the excellence of Israel, For the emptiers have emptied them out And ruined their vine branches. **(Nahum 2:1, 2 NKJV)**

7. Lord, we don't want anymore bloodshed in _____ (name the city) through gun violence or terrorism. We rise up

and slay all the enemies in the high places and we employ your warrior angels: visit the wicked with your militant angels, let none of them escape in Jesus' name.

Then the angel of the Lord went forth, and smote in the camp of the Assyrians a hundred and fourscore and five thousand: and when they arose early in the morning, behold, they were all dead corpses. **(Isaiah 37:36 KJV)**

8. Let your revolution against the wicked be swift! Let your fire fall on _____ to consume every works of darkness. Let the angel of the Lord pursue and destroy them suddenly! NO MORE VIOLENCE! We disallow it in Jesus' name.

Let them be like chaff before the wind, And let the angel of the Lord chase them. Let their way be dark and slippery, And let the angel of the Lord pursue them. Let destruction come upon him unexpectedly, And let his net that he has hidden catch himself; Into that very destruction let him fall. **(Psalm 35:5, 6, 8 NKJV)**

9. Perfect that which concerns my city or my nation. Separate the righteous from the wicked; do not let the innocent suffer with them on the day of their calamity. Heal our land through righteousness; exalt our nation in Jesus' name.

10. COMMUNION: Father Lord, baptize me with the fire of an intercessor. Let me move nations and shake kingdoms for your glory like Moses and Elijah. Help me to pray selflessly like my Master Jesus. MAKE ME A WORLD CHANGER!

Give thanks for answered prayers!

INSTRUCTION: Go before the Lord at midnight and intercede for your place of origin and your place of residence. Ask the Lord to give you a voice in that land.

DAY 19

YOKE BREAKERS

Today is the nineteenth day of the fast and the Bible says in **Luke 10:19**,

Behold, I give you the authority to trample on serpents and scorpions, and over all the power of the enemy, and nothing shall by any means hurt you.

You have been given the power to walk all over the forces of darkness and destroy every yoke. That is why we are looking at YOKE BREAKERS today. Do you know that spiritual warfare is real? If you look closely at **Luke 10:19**, the preceding verse 18 says, *I saw satan fall like lightning from heaven.* To deal with satanic forces, you must be of a higher rank and you must know it. Lightning is not something you want to mess with but did you know you are made of even tougher stuff? Jesus Himself is the Light of the world and He exudes lightning from His robes.

Luke 9:28-29 in the AMPLIFIED version,

Now about eight days after these teachings, Jesus took with Him Peter and John and James and went up on the mountain to pray. And as He was praying, the appearance of His

countenance became altered different, and His raiment became dazzling white flashing with the brilliance of lightning.

Combine that with the revelation knowledge in **John 1:1-5&9,**

In the beginning was the Word, and the Word was with God, and the Word was God. He was in the beginning with God. All things were made through Him, and without Him nothing was made that was made. In Him was life, and the life was the light of men. And the light shines in the darkness, and the darkness did not comprehend it. That was the true Light which gives light to every man coming into the world.

Revelation 1:13-16 describes Him this way,

And in the midst of the lampstands One like a Son of Man, clothed with a robe which reached to His feet and with a girdle of gold about His breast. His head and His hair were white like white wool, as white as snow, and His eyes flashed like a flame of fire. His feet glowed like burnished bright bronze as it is refined in a furnace, and His voice was like the sound of many waters. In His right hand He held seven stars, and from His mouth there came forth a sharp two-edged sword, and His face was like the sun shining in full power at midday.

Does this ring a bell? Do you remember Him as the fourth man in the fiery furnace in Daniel 3:25, *"Look!" The king answered, "I see four men loose, walking in the midst of the fire; and they are not hurt, and the form of the fourth is like the Son of God."* He is the Fourth Man in the fire! He is the Fire in the burning bush!! His the Consuming Fire!!! Stop looking at Jesus like an ordinary man or a weak master. He is far from being weak or small. He is greater than the greatest. He fills up the whole universe! Even the demons know who He is and they tremble.

I want to paint a different picture of the CAPTAIN OF THE HOST who never fails! He is the ANOINTING THAT BREAKS THE YOKE! When the forces of darkness throw you into the fire, He does not leave you stranded there; He goes in with you. He knows how to show up in that kind of space. He is the One who protects you such that the smell of fire will not even be found on you.

Daniel 3:27,

> *And the satraps, administrators, governors, and the king's counselors gathered together, and they saw these men on whose bodies the fire had no power; the hair of their head was not singed nor were their garments affected, and the smell of fire was not on them.*

Have you lit a candle before or burnt a little piece of paper? Can you smell it? Okay, have you cooked anything before and it got burnt a little? Can you smell the burnt offering? How much more when your barbecue grill goes on overdrive, can you smell the smoke on the feast? It is not palatable at all. So imagine, if you will, three men thrown into a mega-sized oven and they came out untouched and their hair or clothes were not burnt nor the smell of fire on them! That is the God we serve!!

If you look closely at the man Elijah, he dealt with satanic forces cheaply because he was supernaturally empowered. After this fast, you should not just be leaner but you should be calling fire down to burn up witchcraft forces like Elijah did to the wicked cohort of Jezebel in 1 Kings 18. Because you carry a higher power and fire, whenever you show up their altar becomes void and dead. You may have shed a lot of physical weight but you must have gained a lot of spiritual weight. Not only that, you would have contacted unquenchable fire from this mountain. The fire that licks up water. This fire licks up the filthy water of sicknesses and diseases. This fire licks up bad blood and frailty in your body. This fire purifies and gives life to all that is consecrated to the Lord. This fire is unkillable and unquenchable!

You should be roasting up monitoring spirits like Elijah did in **2 Kings 1:9-15**. I declare that after this fast, not only will you be calling down fire from heaven through your prayers, you will command angelic presence. The forces of darkness will bow down before you in Jesus' name! The man Elijah by this anointing of fire was able to defeat lack and want. His anointing broke the yoke of poverty and made a laughing stock of famine. This anointing does not respect any global recession. Because Elijah walked with the Lord, he not only enjoyed divine provision but carried it with him everywhere he went. He personally ate angel's food. He affected the family of the widow of Zarephath with abundance and finally impacted a nation's economy. You are cut from the same cloth as Elijah – you are a powerhouse and a resource center. Through the Spirit that raised Jesus from the dead that indwells you, you are a demon chaser and yoke breaker like Christ Jesus! If this fast does not bring out the lion in you, then I wonder what will. Observing the prayer watches and studying the word in this fast must release your true nature to your world. The fleshly wrap must be done away with to reveal the spirit man hidden within – the true you must show up. The world is waiting for the manifestation of the sons of Elohim. You will no longer fight as one who beats empty air. You have been supernaturally enabled on this mountain; go and set the captives free. You are the light that exposes the works of darkness now. You are not only a snake whisperer but a demon chaser – a world changer.

You speak, and they tremble!

Look at the man Moses, the Lord started by introducing him to raw power. He made him face his fears by picking up a snake by its tail. **Exodus 4:3-4,**

> *And He said, "Cast it on the ground." So he cast it on the ground, and it became a serpent; and Moses fled from it. Then the Lord said to Moses, "Reach out your hand and take it by the tail" and he reached out his hand and caught it, and it became a rod in his hand.*

You may not know it but touching a snake by its tail is not a logical thing to do. But God told Moses to do it - He taught him so well that his snake swallowed up the snakes of all the magicians and diviners in Egypt. God can get spooky with the spooky. He knows how to pay the wicked back in their own coin. Go and read through all the plagues that He afflicted Egypt with in **Exodus 7:11 & 22,**

> *But Pharaoh also called the wise men and the sorcerers; so the magicians of Egypt, also did in like manner with their enchantments all that Moses has done.*

They could copy the real thing! Don't get it mixed up – Satan is the copycat. God was just paying them back in their own coin and with the final plague He showed them that there is a higher power! A power you can't mess with. He killed the firstborn in every single household without lifting up a finger.

Are there enchantments or sorcery arrayed against you - today that power is shattered! Are there unrepentant adversaries contesting your victory and liberty before this fast? I declare that they will receive the shock of their lives this midnight in Jesus' name. Go through the scriptures thoroughly and you will see that God can employ anything to defend His own. He rained hail and thunder mixed with fire on Egypt in **Exodus 9:28-29** that Pharaoh began to beg for mercy; he said,

Entreat the Lord, that there may be no more mighty thundering and hail, for it is enough. I will let you go, and you shall stay no longer." So Moses said to him, "As soon as I have gone out of the city, I will spread out my hands to the Lord; the thunder will cease, and there will be no more hail, that you may know that the earth is the Lord's.

THE LORD WILL HUMILIATE ALL YOUR STUBBORN ENEMIES TODAY IN JESUS' NAME.

When our Lord Jesus came down from the Mountain of Transfiguration in **Mark 9:25**, He rebuked the unclean spirit, saying to it: "Deaf and dumb spirit, I command you, come out of him and enter him no more!" Jesus broke the demonic yoke of affliction easily and when the disciples asked him why they could not do it in verse 28 & 29, He said it was because of their unbelief. He said unbelief (doubt) does not go out easily but by fasting and prayer. Praying and fasting grows your faith and helps you to operate the sixth sense which we have established is superior to the five senses. Just like our Lord Jesus Christ, as you come down from this mountain, demons will tremble before you. Your midnight watch will move the earth like Paul and Silas; and chains of affliction will begin to give way in Jesus' mighty name.

For someone reading this book, today is your day of deliverance from that longstanding affliction – you have come to the right mountain today!

Obadiah 1:17-18,

"But on Mount Zion there shall be deliverance, And there shall be holiness; The house of Jacob shall possess their possessions.

The house of Jacob shall be a fire, And the house of Joseph a flame; But the house of Esau shall be stubble; They shall kindle them and devour them, And no survivor shall remain of the house of Esau,"For the Lord has spoken.

Receive this fire in Jesus' name! You will no longer go to bed scared or wake up afraid. You will operate the anointing that breaks every yoke according to **Isaiah 10:27**,

It shall come to pass in that day That his burden will be taken away from your shoulder, And his yoke from your neck, And the yoke will be destroyed because of the anointing.

Some Bible versions add (oil).

Did you know you can anoint anything and anyone to break evil yokes? Moses was instructed by God to do it and the same is confirmed in **James 5:14**,

Is anyone among you afflicted or sick? Let him call for the elders of the church, and let them pray over him, anointing him with oil in the name of the Lord.

You can destroy satanic afflictions through the anointed one and His anointing according to **Acts 10:38**,

How God anointed and consecrated Jesus of Nazareth with the Holy Spirit and with strength and ability and power; how He went about doing good and, in particular, curing all who were harassed and oppressed by the power of the devil, for God was with Him.

GO AND BREAK THOSE YOKES OF HARASSMENT AND OPPRESSION IN HIS NAME.

For you to manifest this power that breaks evil yokes, you must be conscious of the power you carry. For you to defeat any satanic lightning, you must understand that you operate by the authority higher than theirs. That power is only known to be in Christ Jesus. He has disarmed and triumphed over them completely. You can break that marital yoke today by His anointing. You can destroy that yoke of poverty, lack and shame by the anointing. You can break every demonic yoke and shatter that generational yoke of affliction that runs in your bloodline. GO AND CHANGE YOUR WORLD!

It is time to pray.

DAY 19 PRAYER POINTS:

1. Thank You Lord for complete victory over every works of darkness. Thank You for translating me from darkness into Your marvelous light.

2. Thank You for the gift of life and family. I am grateful for letting me triumph daily in Christ even when I walk through the fire and through the waters.

3. Thank You for showing me the secrets of a yoke breaker on this Mountain of Transfiguration. Thank You for making me stronger and wiser in this fast.

4. I operate with the authority to trample on serpents and scorpions and the fullness of the power to walk all over the forces of darkness. I am an enforcer of the yoke-breaking anointing of Jesus Christ over my family, city and nation.

5. From this mountain, I emerge a demon chaser and yoke breaker. I manifest as the light of the world and darkness flees before me in Jesus' name. I am empowered to break prisoners free on a daily basis!

6. I am unstoppable, unquenchable and unkillable because greater is He that lives in me than he that lives in the world. I go in the spirit and power of Elijah. I am too hot for the enemy to handle. I am God's BATTLE-AXE!

7. From today, every satanic yoke in my household is destroyed and no demonic affliction is permitted in my life. I speak to the situation of _____ (ungodly delay, barrenness, generational poverty, genetic illnesses, marital problems, repeated failure, evil trends, limitation and stagnation, disappointment and defeat, abortion of destiny, strange battles, sorcery and divination, witchcraft forces etc.)

8. Today, I possess my possession on this mountain! I take back all that was stolen from me by the enemy. I take back my _____(portion, anointing, increase, destiny, children) with interest like Moses; I catch up and overtake all those who have gone ahead of me like Elijah in the name of Jesus.

9. I operate in the miraculous and walk in the supernatural like Moses and Elijah. The same anointing that heals the sick and sets the oppressed free in working in me for the deliverance of my generation in Jesus' name. I harass the harasser and oppress the oppressor!

10. COMMUNION: From this table I tap into the anointing of fire that breaks every yoke. My body, receive fire; my soul, contact fire; my spirit, become fire – the Refiner's fire, refine me. Purifying Fire, purify me. Consuming Fire, consume me for exploits in Jesus' name.

Give thanks for answered prayers!

INSTRUCTION: At midnight, call on the Lord of Host to finish all your unfinished battles. Make sure you take your list. Go before Him with praises and exit with thanksgiving.

DAY 20

SONS ARE HERE

Today is the twentieth day of the fast and the topic is SONS ARE HERE. The number twenty represents the age of maturity into sonship.

Romans 8:19,
> *"For the earnest expectation of the creation eagerly waits for the revealing (manifestation) of the sons of God" (emphasis mine).*

Twenty is the age of manifestation! Twenty is the age where sons are enlisted for warfare in Israel according to **Numbers 1:3,**
> *From twenty years old and above—all who are able to go to war in Israel. You and Aaron shall number them by their armies.*

You have been numbered among sons from today; you have what it takes to handle spiritual warfare. You are equipped for your destiny and you will not turn back from your assignment like the children of Ephraim in **Psalm 78:9,**
> *The children of Ephraim, being armed and carrying bows, Turned back in the day of battle.*

Note that the Bible refers to them as children not sons. Why? The following verses show us the reason why they failed. The children of Ephraim failed because verses 10-11 say,

> *They did not keep the covenant of God; They refused to walk in His law, And forgot His works And His wonders that He had shown them.*

(1) They did not keep the covenant

(2) They refused to walk

(3) They forgot what He had shown them

After engaging in this fast, please keep the covenant with the Lord in all ramifications. Walk in all His ways that you learnt on this mountain and remember all the secrets He has shown you. Keep the prayer watches - that was the secret of Jesus and the other two we studied extensively in this fast. Fast regularly on your own, please don't be a child about spiritual things anymore – a son will fast a least once a week but a child will wait to be told by a parent or teacher to do it once in a while with the whole church. You must operate with understanding like the sons of Issachar in **1 Chronicles 12:32**,

> *Of the sons of Issachar who had understanding of the times, to know what Israel ought to do, their chiefs were two hundred; and all their brethren were at their command.*

What put them in command was the understanding they had.

This is the time where you leave childish things behind and begin to handle matters of adulthood. No wonder modern civilization and cultures acknowledges individuals as adults from age 21 as fully grown adults, who are capable of making decisions without parental consent.

Paul said in **1 Corinthians 13:11**,

> *When I was a child, I spoke as a child, I understood as a child, I thought as a child; but when I became a man, I put away childish things.*

It is time for many of us on this line to manifest sonship in the place of prayer. **Galatians 4:1-7** describes the difference between a child and a son. Some people are content with being a child of God but a child cannot handle the full inheritance of His father, he may enjoy some things that his guardians and stewards give to him but it is not until full maturity into sonship that he can own it. Is there something still missing in your life right now? It is time to grow up into sonship.

Please grow up and know your rights in the Lord – you have been exiled enough! You are not a regent but the real deal. You are a royal priesthood and a holy nation called to display God's glory. STOP LIVING A LIFE OF DEPRIVATION! **Galatians 4:1-7** says,

> *Now I say that the heir, as long as he is a child, does not differ at all from a slave, though he is master of all, but is under guardians and stewards until the time appointed by the father. Even so we, when we were children, were in bondage under the elements of the world. But when the fullness of the time had come, God sent forth His Son, born of a woman, born under the law, to redeem those who were under the law, that we might receive the adoption as sons. And because you are sons, God has sent forth the Spirit of His Son into your hearts, crying out, "Abba, Father!" Therefore you are no longer a slave but a son, and if a son, then an heir of God through Christ. You are joint heirs with Him. It is time to enter into that inheritance.*

On the Mountain of Transfiguration, we see that the Father openly acknowledges Jesus Christ as His son. Sons hear the voice of the Father with clarity – just like the two men Elijah and Moses. When you hear the voice of the Lord the Author of Life Himself, you can speak to any dead situation and it will come alive. I want you to know that sometimes when the voice of the Lord openly approves you, the devil will test you. He wants to know if you are made of the real stuff like the true sons of God. Our Lord Jesus was tested this way too. He was acknowledged by God in **Matthew 3:16-17,**

> *When He had been baptized, Jesus came up immediately from the water; and behold, the heavens were opened to Him, and He saw the Spirit of God descending like a dove and alighting upon Him. And suddenly a voice came from heaven, saying, "This is My beloved Son, in whom I am well pleased."*

But in **Matthew 4:1**, he was tempted by the devil,

> *Then Jesus was led up by the Spirit into the wilderness to be tempted by the devil.*

Don't be afraid of tests or trials – they are the furnaces where testimonies and triumphs are created. The silver and the gold go through rigor to come out with the splendor they reflect. The approval of God over your life attracts trials and temptation. Embrace it and rejoice when you see them because without a test there is no testimony; trials always end in triumph. Job was tested but at the end he received ten times more than he ever had. When Jesus was tried and tested, he became a walking sign and wonder according to Acts 10:38.

James 1:2-4,

> *My brethren, count it all joy when you fall into various trials, knowing that the testing of your faith produces patience. But*

let patience have its perfect work, that you may be perfect and complete, lacking nothing.

Trials perfect you. Stop despising them; trials mature you and polish you. They develop your character and make you unshakeable and immoveable. Just like in school where before every promotion there is a test, so also in life the test leads to your testimony.

Job 23:10,

> *But He knows the way that I take; When He has tested me, I shall come forth as gold.*

The test is a divine process to grow you, groom you and perfect you.

The voice of the Lord is only clear to those who have a deeper walk with him. Those who hunger and thirst after righteousness – those who pant after Him like the deer pants after the water brook; those who seek Him at the prayer watches, those who hide in the secret place of the Most High studying, meditating, praying and praising; those who have removed the noise to hear His voice; those who have removed themselves from every distraction to seek Him as the center of attraction. When Jesus prayed publicly to the Father in **John 12:28-29**, the sons heard the voice of the Father clearly but others heard thunder,

> *"…Father, glorify Your name." Then a voice came from heaven, saying, "I have both glorified it and will glorify it again." Therefore the people who stood by and heard it said that it had thundered. Others said, "An angel has spoken to Him."*

Jesus got the divine approval on the Mount of Transfiguration in **Luke 9:29,**

> *As He prayed, the appearance of His face was altered, and His robe became white and glistening.*

He was supernaturally empowered to face his divine destiny as the sacrifice that will atone for the sins of the entire world. I declare that is how everyone who has been praying and seeking God's face on this mountain will become transfigured and transformed. You will be supernaturally empowered to fulfill your destiny and manifest God's glory to your world. The multitude came to meet him to heal and deliver them. Your life will be transformed and your generation will celebrate God's deposit into your life. You will echo His voice through the uttermost parts of the earth in Jesus' name!

Do you know you can hear that voice today according to **Hebrews 1:1-2**?

Hebrews 1:2,
> *...has in these last days spoken to us by His Son, whom He has appointed heir of all things, through whom also He made the worlds;*

By the help of the Holy Spirit you can hear the inaudible according **Isaiah 30:21**,
> *Your ears shall hear a word behind you, saying, "This is the way, walk in it," Whenever you turn to the right hand Or whenever you turn to the left. And from the pages of scriptures you can see the invisible.*

God has called you out as sons. He wants you to display his divine nature because you were made in His image and after His likeness. What is the difference between sons and children? It is definitely not age according to **Job 32:7-9**,
> *I said, 'Age should speak, And multitude of years should teach*

wisdom.' But there is a spirit in man, And the breath of the Almighty gives him understanding. Great men are not always wise, Nor do the aged always understand justice.

It is clear that at New Birth we become born again and the Bible calls us new born babes. How do we then move from childhood to sonship? It is easy to deduce from the life of Jesus - in **Luke 2:52**,

And Jesus increased in wisdom and stature, and in favor with God and men.

He had to grow spirit, soul and body. In all three areas! Like Jesus, you must grow in your spirit and your soul. Many believers have the body of a 30 year old but the soul of an infant – they are completely stunted and a bundle of contradiction.

You are no ordinary person; stop looking at yourself as just flesh and bones. You have supernatural life dwelling in you and have royal blood flowing in your veins. You carry the DNA of the Most High God in you; you have the molecule of life resident in you. You are a divine monarch. The Bible says in John 3:31 that He who comes from above is above all; he who is of the earth is earthly and speaks of the earth. He who comes from heaven is above all. When you understand who you are in Christ, kings will respect and acknowledge you. They will pay homage to you.

Isaiah 60:1&3,

Arise, shine; For your light has come! And the glory of the Lord is risen upon you. The Gentiles shall come to your light, And kings to the brightness of your rising.

When you know who you are in Christ, demons will bow before you as they did before Christ Jesus. As He stepped out of the presence of the Father, all the forces of darkness could not stand in His presence. They trembled and fled out of their hiding places. You will walk in the reality of that power from today in Jesus' name. You are the solution your neighborhood is waiting for. You can command abundant provision like Elijah and Moses wherever you show up. You will bring divine restoration on all fronts in your family and to all those around you. You will possess your possessions on this mountain of deliverance.

> *The threshing floors will be full of wheat, And the vats shall overflow with new wine and oil. "So the Lord will restore to you the years that the swarming locust has eaten, The crawling locust, The consuming locust, And the chewing locust, My great army which I sent among you. You shall eat in plenty and be satisfied.*

As you have learnt the secrets of praise on this mountain, you can praise the name of the Lord your God into the realm of wondrous works! You can praise that situation of shame and reproach to become honor and glory; you can praise down a rain of favor and grace! You can pray your city into a spiritual revival! You can engage the young and the old in your community for righteousness. You can heal the sick and deliver the oppressed. You have been empowered to harass the harasser!

As a son, you will begin to walk in a realm of daily exploits and revelations in the spirit. Instructive and revelational dreams will become your nature like that of Moses. You will become a rain maker like Elijah, commanding fire and hail on the kingdom of darkness! He said in **Joel 2**,

> *And I will show wonders in the heavens and in the earth: Blood and fire and pillars of smoke. The sun shall be turned into*

darkness, And the moon into blood, Before the coming of the great and awesome day of the Lord.

The day of the Lord is at hand! He wants to intimate us about the details of His return. And we are the ones He is calling to usher in that season. We will not be caught sleeping as dumb watchmen – we must be alert on our watch! As a son of the Most High, you can command global attention like our Lord Jesus Christ but you will have to open your mouth to issue those decrees and pronounce the judgement in the place of prayer.

If you are saved, then you are part of this formidable end-time army described in **Joel 2:1-5 & 10**,

Blow the trumpet in Zion, And sound an alarm in My holy mountain! Let all the inhabitants of the land tremble; For the day of the Lord is coming, For it is at hand: A day of darkness and gloominess, A day of clouds and thick darkness, Like the morning clouds spread over the mountains. A people come, great and strong, The like of whom has never been; Nor will there ever be any such after them, Even for many successive generations. A fire devours before them, And behind them a flame burns; The land is like the Garden of Eden before them, And behind them a desolate wilderness; Surely nothing shall escape them. Their appearance is like the appearance of horses; And like swift steeds, so they run. With a noise like chariots Over mountaintops they leap, Like the noise of a flaming fire that devours the stubble, Like a strong people set in battle array...the earth quakes before them and the heavens tremble.

WHAT A MAGNIFICENT BREED! What an awesome display of power!! What a great army! A terror to the forces of darkness! A great reformation and a massive revival this is!

The Lord is calling out for sons today. He wants to empower you for destiny. Will you let Him use you in that capacity? He wants you to step into power from obscurity. He wants you to put on strength like never before. Sons of Elohim, ARISE!!

It is time to pray.

DAY 20 PRAYER POINTS

1. Thank You Lord for the precious blood of the Lamb that bought me from the bondage of sin and transformed me into a son.

2. Thank You for the Spirit of sonship whereby we cry Abba, Father and for making me a joint heir with Christ Jesus. Thank You for transforming me from childhood to sonship and for maturing me to take hold of my inheritance in you.

3. Thank You for life, safety and good health. Thank You for my family and loved ones. Thank You for supplying all my needs according to your riches in glory by Christ Jesus.

4. Father Lord, as I walk into the reality of my sonship through Christ Jesus, I wax strong in the spirit and I grow daily in wisdom and have favor with God and men. I mature spirit, soul and body.

5. This is my season of manifestation as I reveal the glory of the Lord to my generation. I walk in dominion and power healing the sick and setting the captives free. I am a walking bundle of miracle, signs and wonder in Jesus' name.

6. From this Mountain of Transfiguration, I am transformed into the same image of the Son of God. I manifest hegemony, command, mastery, control, sway, authority and the like. I operate with the boldness and anointing of the Lion of Judah.

7. Like the sons of Issachar, I demonstrate understanding and I have the details of my assignment on the earth per time. I defeat all the forces of procrastination and I run my race with divine speed in Jesus' name.

8. From today, I keep the covenant of the Lord and walk in all His ways; I engage the prayer watches and operate by the secrets He has shown me on this mountain. I will labor in prayer, praises and the word; I will fast on a regular basis to renew my spiritual strength in Jesus' name.

9. Father Lord, strengthen me for spiritual battles and empower me for greater exploits. I refuse to turn back like the children of Ephraim but I run ahead with your fire like the Joel 2 army – my strength will not fail and my vision will not grow dim.

10. COMMUNION: From this table, I contact the anointing of permanent conquest like my Master Jesus. Announce me to my world as your son and use me to display your glory. Let me command global attention for you!

Give thanks for answered prayers!

INSTRUCTION: At midnight, pray your way into God's will for your life and destiny. Pray in tongues for 30 minutes. He will speak to you (Make sure you go before Him with a notepad and a pen to write down the vision).

DAY 21

PRAISE STORM

Congratulations! You have made it by His grace. The twenty-one days of fasting and praying have finally come to an end and you have gained victory over all the issues that brought you before the Lord. Like Daniel, you have been heard! Your petitions have been granted and your warfare accomplished. The angel of the Lord appeared to Daniel in **Daniel 10:12-14**,

> *Saying "Do not fear, Daniel, for from the first day that you set your heart to understand, and to humble yourself before your God, your words were heard; and I have come because of your words. But the prince of the kingdom of Persia withstood me twenty-one days; and behold, Michael, one of the chief princes, came to help me, for I had been left alone there with the kings of Persia. Now I have come to make you understand what will happen to your people in the latter days, for the vision refers to many days yet to come."*

I have good news for you, the moment you made up your mind to build this 21 days altar unto the Lord, He heard you already.

Today is not just a day of prayer but a day of exuberant praise! You are storming the gates of heaven with praise! The Lord Jesus Himself teaching us the fundamental secrets of three things done in the secret that provokes divine reward in the book of Matthew 6 – **Matthew 6:3, 6 &17**:

(1) when you give

(2) when you pray

(3) when you fast

You have done all three on this mountain following the perfect example of our Lord Jesus Christ. He said our Father who sees all these things in the secret will reward us in the open. You are guaranteed your divine reward in Jesus' name. You have been instructed to sow during this fast (see the instruction for Day 14). You have prayed fervently daily and have also fasted for twenty-one days. The only thing left for you to do as you await the open reward is to praise Him.

Solomon, after he offered a thousand burnt offering to the Lord, the heavens opened and he got a blank check in **1 Kings 3:4-5**,

> Now the king went to Gibeon to sacrifice there, for that was the great high place: Solomon offered a thousand burnt offerings on that altar. At Gibeon the Lord appeared to Solomon in a dream by night; and God said, "Ask! What shall I give you?"

Likewise, you will get your own blank check from the Lord today in Jesus' mighty name.

You are going to provoke a better encounter here on this altar through a PRAISE STORM because Christ said a better than Solomon is here. Go and get your dancing shoes on because you are going to offer Him your own thousand offering – the

Bible calls it the sacrifice of praise in **Hebrews 13:15**,
> *Therefore by Him let us continually offer the sacrifice of praise to God, that is, the fruit of our lips, giving thanks to His name.*

You will wrap up the fast with a Praise Storm. Because when praises go up, His blessings come down. Remember **Psalm 67:5-7**,
> *Let the peoples praise You, O God; Let all the peoples praise You. Then the earth shall yield her increase; God, our own God, shall bless us. God shall bless us, And all the ends of the earth shall fear Him.*

Get ready because like Elijah, I hear the sound of abundance of rain! What happened before the rain – an altar was built for the Lord and the sacrifice was offered and fire fell from heaven. Come on now! We have built an altar unto the Lord and have been offering our sacrifice of praise for the past twenty-one days. It is time to experience the rain of blessings.

The glory cloud descended in **2 Chronicles 7:1-3**,
> *When Solomon had finished praying, fire came down from heaven and consumed the burnt offering and the sacrifices; and the glory of the Lord filled the temple. And the priests could not enter the house of the Lord, because the glory of the Lord had filled the Lord's house. When all the children of Israel saw how the fire came down, and the glory of the Lord on the temple, they bowed their faces to the ground on the pavement, and worshiped and praised the Lord, saying: "For He is good, For His mercy endures forever."*

You are experiencing the same glory cloud today on this mountain! And the glory cloud has come to stay with you forever.

Every generational curse is turned supernaturally to blessings – like the sons of Korah who had a different covenant with the Lord because of their heart of praise. Their father had perished when he attacked Moses with his unscrupulous company of friends, Datham and Abiram.

Numbers 16:32,
And the earth opened its mouth and swallowed them up, with their households and all the men with Korah, with all their goods.

The ground swallowed them up but if you look through the book of Psalm and everywhere praise is mentioned, the sons of Korah were mentioned, they did not carry the curse placed on their father's house. They were a different breed because of praise. You can start a new breed for the Lord in your family from that altar of praise. No more failure at the edge of success. No more barrenness. No more ungodly delay. No more sickness passed down through the generations. No more demonic afflictions. No more idols.

The Sons of Korah wrote many Psalms like **Psalm 46:1-11**,
God is our refuge and strength, A very present help in trouble. Therefore we will not fear, Even though the earth be removed, And though the mountains be carried into the midst of the sea; Though its waters roar and be troubled, Though the mountains shake with its swelling. Selah. There is a river whose streams shall make glad the city of God, The holy place of the tabernacle of the Most High. God is in the midst of her, she shall not be moved; God shall help her, just at the break of dawn. The nations raged, the kingdoms were moved; He uttered His voice, the earth melted. The Lord of hosts is with us; The God of Jacob is our refuge. Selah. Come, behold the works of the Lord,

Who has made desolations in the earth. He makes wars cease to the end of the earth;He breaks the bow and cuts the spear in two; He burns the chariot in the fire. Be still, and know that I am God; I will be exalted among the nations, I will be exalted in the earth! The Lord of hosts is with us; The God of Jacob is our refuge. Selah.

I love the song in **Psalm 48:1-2**,

Great is the Lord, and greatly to be praised In the city of our God, In His holy mountain. Beautiful in elevation, The joy of the whole earth, Is Mount Zion on the sides of the north, The city of the great King.

They tell us to recount the blessings of the Lord in **Psalm 48:12-13**,

Walk about Zion, And go all around her. Count her towers; Mark well her bulwarks; Consider her palaces; That you may tell it to the generation following.

And it ends with the popular song in **Psalm 48:14**,

For this is God,Our God forever and ever; He will be our guide Even unto the end.

When the altar of the Lord is in your home, there are explosive blessings. Like what happened in **2 Samuel 6:11-15**,

The Ark of the Lord remained there in Obed-edom's house for three months, and the Lord blessed Obed-edom and his entire household. Then King David was told, "The Lord has blessed Obed-edom's household and everything he has because of the Ark of God." So David went there and brought the Ark of God from the house of Obed-edom to the City of David with a great celebration. After the men who were carrying the Ark of the Lord had gone six steps, David sacrificed a bull and a

> *fattened calf. And David danced before the Lord with all his might, wearing a priestly garment. So David and all the people of Israel brought up the Ark of the Lord with shouts of joy and the blowing of rams' horns.*

David was a very smart king, he went to bring the same altar to the city. He danced like a crazy man to provoke God's favor. He built a tabernacle of praise – a mobile tent, every six steps he took he offered a sacrifice of praise. Can you offer your own sacrifice of praise? Can you give the Lord the glory due to His name regardless of the fact that the man you want to marry has not shown up yet or the promotion you want is not here yet or that baby you have been trying to carry is not yet conceived? Can you offer Him preceding praise for what you have not yet seen in the physical but is already manifested in the spirit realm. Is it okay to give to Him succeeding praise for the breath in you and the gift of life? Can you praise Him that you are not even in the asylum? Can you praise Him that you even made it out alive from that surgery, whether minor or major – He still sustained you. It means He is not done with you yet.

Do you know that is what brings down the glory cloud of His presence? The Psalmist said in **Psalm 16:11**,

> *You will show me the path of life; In Your presence is fullness of joy; At Your right hand are pleasures forevermore.*

Those things you are looking for everywhere is right there in His presence. If I were you, I will do all it takes to get into that presence and stay there. Praise is the key into His presence. Psalm 100:4 says *I will enter his gates with thanksgiving and into His courts with praise.* Sing a new song to him today. Permit me to misbehave a little like David. When I praise the Lord, I lose all comportment and decorum. The majesty and honor is for

Him alone. When you have sufficiently provoked the glory cloud, you will step down from this mountain empowered and the entire world will glorify the Lord with you. The demons will bow before you and the crowd will cheer on your behalf like in **Luke 9:43**,

> *The crowd began cheering and discussing this amazing healing and the power of God...*
> (The Voice)

Awe will grip the people as they see the majestic display of God's power over your life.

Luke 9:43,
> *Awe gripped the people as they saw this majestic display of God's power. While everyone was marveling at everything he was doing (New Living Translation).*

Those who knew you before will be astonished at the evidence of God's mighty power and His majesty and magnificence over you in Jesus' name.

PRAISE HIM IN YOUR OWN WAY:

The First and the Last
The Beginning and the End
The One who has been before the beginning began
The Ageless One
The Ancient of Days that never grows bald nor wrinkles...

The General Superintendent of the whole galaxies
The Master of the Universe
Captain of the Cosmos
The Creator of Heaven and Earth
The Possessor of Heaven and Earth

The Heaven is His Throne and the earth his footstool
The Governor among nations
The Prime minister of all prime ministers
The King of kings
The Lord of lords

7 PRAISE POINTS:

1. Thank You Lord for the wondrous works You have done on this mountain of transfiguration these past 21 days.

2. Thank You for the revelation knowledge and eye opening experience in the word. Thank You for sharing divine secrets with me.

3. Thank You for the miraculous healing and deliverance from household wickedness. Thank You for new babies, marriages, jobs, promotions and enlargement.

4. Thank You for teaching us about the prayer watches and for showing us the power in the night watches. Thank You for permanent victories won by the blood of Jesus.

5. Thank You Lord for the past few months and the mysteries locked away in the remaining months of the year.

6. Thank You Lord for the transformation that has taken place on this mountain, especially for empowering my destiny for fulfillment.

7. COMMUNION: Thank You Lord for the outpouring anointing of a watchman and the yoke breaking anointing of my Lord Jesus Christ. Thank You for perfecting anointing of this day.

7 PROPHETIC WORDS

(1) You will gain uncommon speed in destiny - you will catch up with those who have gone ahead of you and overtake them.

(2) All that you could not achieve in the past by human strength, you will do it with excellence after this unusual fast.

(3) As you follow the instruction from the beginning of this fast, you will have uncommon breakthroughs in Jesus' name.

(4) Many celebrations of double perfection babies are lined up for the next year.

(5) For the singles – every month of the next year you will be witnessing one marriage after another and yours will be one of them in Jesus' name

(6) You will record a notable testimony each month for the rest of your life.

(7) Every request you brought before the Lord on this altar is granted in Jesus' name.

Like Moses and Elijah, your generation will celebrate you. And like our Lord Jesus Christ, you will manifest the Father's glory. Amen!

INSTRUCTION: At midnight, go before the Lord praising Him for each of the seven items on your list.
**Remember to pay your vow to the Lord.

CONCLUSION
THE GOD LIFE AWAKENS

As you must have seen through the pages of this book that fasting unveils the life within, it awakens the God life in you. It reveals the true nature of God on your inside. It unravels the genetic code of the Most High from your spirit man. Your supernatural DNA becomes evident and works in full force. Our Father is Spirit and we can only gain access to Him as spirits according to **John 4:24**. The key to unlocking your spiritual DNA and living as a true son of Elohim is to engage the key of fasting and prayer on a regular basis.

Fasting mortifies your flesh and empowers your spirit man. Fasting makes you SUPER-natural, you cease to depend on the natural strength that comes from physical food but now gain surpassing strength from spiritual food. You stop hearing with your physical ears but start hearing from the realm of the spirit, you begin to tap into the realm of the inaudible. When you fast, you will stop thinking with your natural mind but will now start to perceive with your spiritual mind - your heart. You will stop making decision based on human logic or reasoning in the flesh but will start being led by the Spirit. You will not only stop walking by the five physical senses - but will start operating by the sixth sense (the spirit of faith).

Your fasting will silence the physical senses for the spirit of faith to flow through with clarity. This is what happens when a born again christian fasts - i.e. every recreated human spirit that has been regenerated by the blood of Jesus. The Spirit that raised Christ from the dead will quicken you tremendously (**Romans 8:11**) and it will show in every area of your life. At first, you may be the only one who notices the change in your life but believe me with the passage of time, the world will notice that you carry a different spirit and operate from a higher dimension.

This confirms the word of God in **Matthew 6:17-18** that says when you fast in the secret, your Father who sees you in the secret will reward you openly. There is no way you fast according to scriptural prescription that it will not show after a while. Like our Master Jesus, your face will shine with undeniable glory and your youth will be renewed in the order of Moses who lived to be a hundred and twenty years old but his physical body refused to die until God took him. The face of the man Moses shone with such glory that no one could look him in the face after he had spent forty days on the mountain with the Lord. When you engage the fasting key the anointing and intensity of fire power that you carry within will come shining through.

It will flow effortlessly such that demons will come running out of their hide-outs without you raising your voice and you will sweatlessly heal the sick. The anointing to set the captives free will be readily available for you to do exploits with in the order of **Acts 10:38**. This was why the Lord stated emphatically in **Matthew 17:21** that this kind goes not out but by fasting and by prayer. The power is already given by Christ Jesus to every believer, it is not your fasting that gets the power but fasting unleashes the power. Christ paid the full price of redemption with His blood and He gave us the same power and commission on the earth to act in His place. **1 John 4:17b** says, "As He is, so are we in this world" and we know that all power in heaven and earth have been given to Him.

He has given us the mandate to go into all the world and preach the gospel to every creature. He called us to walk in the supernatural and do signs everyday of our existence here on earth. This task is very difficult and almost impossible to a regular human but it becomes a walk-over for the empowered believer. The key to walking in this realm of power is fasting and prayer. It marked the ministry of our Lord Jesus Christ and all through the gospels, we see how He engaged this key effortlessly - He was our perfect example.

Many times, the Bible says that He will go by Himself to a solitary place to pray before others were awake. There were times when He will send the disciples away just to spend time alone with the Father in prayer. His prayer life was so impactful and full of exploits that the disciples asked Him to teach them how to pray. Remember how He gave thanks and food multiplied or when He prayed at the tomb of Lazarus and death gave him up. I personally believe that the Mountain of Transfiguration experience was an insight to his prayer life and how heaven responded to the Son. Our prayer life should be nothing short of this experience on a daily basis. We should grow in the place of prayer such that we are talking to the Father and He is talking back, showing us things to come by the Holy Spirit. The more time we spend in His presence, the more like Him we should become. Prayer and fasting awakens the God life within us - It quickens us!

The truth of the matter is that when you fast you gain supernatural speed and become swift as the eagle. Your spiritual faculties gain acuity because your flesh has been put in the silence mode. Fasting is like the light switch that turns on the super light bulbs of your innermost man according to **Ephesians 1:18,**

> *The eyes of your understanding being enlightened will cause you to know what is the hope of His calling, what are the riches of the glory of His inheritance in the saints.*

Fasting is a key that grants you access into those secrets locked away from the foundations of the world according to **1 Corinthians 2:9-10,**

> *But as it is written:"Eye has not seen, nor ear heard, Nor have entered into the heart of man the things which God has prepared for those who love Him." But God has revealed them to us through His Spirit. For the Spirit searches all things, yes, the deep things of God.*

Your spirit man becomes so empowered that you easily tap into the inheritance already set aside for you in the Kingdom. Fasting opens you up in ways that you can ever imagine. You will begin to have supernatural visions of the day and instructive dreams at night. Just like we see happen on the Mountain of Transfiguration where the Lord Jesus was openly communing with heaven for specific instructions and the Father's voice was heard clearly validating the Son. The experience of Peter, James and John was only an exposure for them to see what the prayer and fasting life of our Lord Jesus Christ was like. He went to show them a preview of what their prayer life must be like when He was no longer with them.

Fasting is not a religious ritual or the fulfillment of a tradition. It is not a rite of passage into the click of the spiritual bigwigs or a boasting right of who can fast the most. It is actually a kingdom key to access the spirit realm. If fasting is done correctly it empowers the individual exponentially but if not done correctly, it can cause more harm to the individual than good. If you fast without studying and meditating on the word with fervent heartfelt prayer, you have successfully engaged in an hunger strike. The fast that is done correctly is the one where you withdraw from all internal and external noise, you must also shut down the noise of social media, mass media and whatever media brings distraction to you. Even a good thing can be a source of distraction a times - e.g. Job, family, business etc. If your job is very tasking or demanding causing distraction from spiritual focus at a time of extended fasting and prayer, you may need to take a few days off the job and settle with the Lord in the secret place to get the best out of the fast. You may still engage in the regular intermittent fast while working or fully engaged with your family but if you are seeking spiritual direction or renewal in an extended fast, please make sure you plan to take some days off to spend alone with the Lord even if it is only a few days out of the entire fast.

The experience of abstaining from food is pointless if you do not substitute the physical food with spiritual food. The word of God is food. It is described as milk, honey, meat and even strong meat. The word of God says that thise who wait on the Lord i.e. Those who fast will mount up with the wings of eagles. Do you know that eagles are not scavengers - they feed on fresh meat dripping with fresh blood. So also is an eagle believer, you never feel satisfied with old stale revelation. You will always hunger and thirst for the fresh revelation of the Most High. Jesus speaking in **Matthew 4:4** and **Luke 4:4** said, man must not live by bread alone but by every word that proceeds out of the mouth of the Lord.

The truth is that no meat compares to the word of God in strength and nourishment. It allows your health to be renewed and strengthens your bones supernaturally. The word of God is called strong meat in **Hebrews 5:13** - it is consumed by sons. Also referred to as milk fed to new born babes in **1 Peter 2:2**. No matter your level in the Lord, you will always find the supernatural food needed for your spiritual nourishment. When you understand this concept of replacing physical food with spiritual food then you will operate effortlessly in the supernatural. You will walk as super-humans with super strength like Elijah who outran a kings chariot because the Lord's hand rested on him.

As you can see from the account of the Mountain of Transfiguration as recorded in **Matthew 17, Luke 9 and Mark 9**. Like our Lord Jesus Christ, fasting will help you to wield that power that unleashes on demons and silences the lions of this world. When the Lord came down from the mountain, He was able to deal mercilessly with the demon that make a mockery of the disciples. He simply cast out the devil that was afflicting the boy without any spiritual gymnastics. You can also walk in this realm of power and unlimited anointing. As a spirit-filled born again child of the Most High, you already carry the same power. **Luke 10:19** confirms that you have power and authority over the works of darkness.

He called you and I to deal with the forces of darkness and has equipped us to set captives free by taking this power bestowed upon us to the world with the mandate of preaching the Kingdom, healing the sick, cleansing the lepers, raising the dead and casting out devils. He showed us this example while on earth and confirmed the same through the pages of scriptures in the Acts of the Apostles. We have the same Spirit and we must take the world by storm with the power that lays dormant that must be awakened to transform our world.

He has called us as yoke breakers, demon chasers and transformers to our world. He has sent us out as ministers of reconciliation to a lost world of humans; He wants us to tell the Adamic race how much He loves man and how mad He is about them. He wants every human to know He is not mad at them but madly in love with them and this love He proved by giving His only Son. Christ died for us and He has called us as superhuman world changers to work the ridiculous miraculous in His name. He is the Lion of the Tribe of Judah who has prevailed and has empowered us as His Lion-kings to defeat the lions of this world. He is the King of Kings and has called us as kings to share His everlasting secrets with us and the whole world is waiting for you and I to manifest as His sons. His formidable army - A terror to the kingdom of darkness as the God life awakens within us. Amen

APPENDIX

NEHEMIAH TROOP BENEDICTION
(Genesis 49:25-26)

I am blessed with the blessing of the Father God Almighty

I am blessed with the blessing of heaven above in Christ Jesus

I am blessed with the blessing of the field

I am blessed with the blessing of the deep within

I am blessed with the blessing of the breast

I am blessed with the blessing of the womb

I am blessed with all spiritual, material and marital blessings this season.

I am blessed when I go out and when I come in

My blessing exceeds that of my ancestors and all those who have gone ahead of me in Jesus mighty name. AMEN.

ABOUT RAENI BANKOLE

Raeni Bankole is a minister of the gospel with a three-fold calling to this generation; she was born and raised in Southern Nigeria as Omolaraeni Odewole in a Christian family of 8 children. She relocated to the United States of America in 2001 to further her education.

In 1997, while studying at the University of Ibadan she heard the first call to be used as a "Repairer of the Breach and a Restorer of the path for men to dwell in" according to Isaiah 58:12. She worked passionately in the campus fellowship at the University of Ibadan and later served as one of the pioneering leaders of the Winners Youth Fellowship of the Living Faith Church (Winners Chapel) till she moved to the United States.

In the United States she has served fervently in several ministries under the Redeemed Christian Church of God for over 12 years in the Chicago-land area till she resumed fulltime ministry in 2013. She currently runs a vibrant prayer school in the Atlanta metro area teaching the word of God and showing the secrets of deliverance. Her passion is to help individuals birth their God-given vision and to nurture those destinies to complete fulfillment. Many of her teachings can be found on Soundcloud.com. She is married to Adebowale Bankole and together they have three children.

Her apostolic calling as a watchman and a voice unto nations operates through different branches of Empowerment Mission Agency (NPF) a registered non-profit organization in the United States of America with a mission to empower nations through Christ.

Mission: Empowering nations through Christ

Vision: Birthing visions and nurturing destinies.

Repairer of the Breach: She teaches and preaches the word of God bringing many to the saving knowledge of the Lord and restoring many lost destinies to their divine destiny in Christ Jesus. "And they shall build the old waste places: you shall raise up the foundations of many generations; and you shall be called, The repairer of the breach, The restorer of paths to dwell in." (Isaiah 58:12).

A Watchman: As a watchman, she runs an intercessory ministry that has a mandate to raise a global army of intercessors unto the kingdom of our Lord Jesus Christ...I have made you a watchman for the house of Israel; therefore you shall hear a word from My mouth and warn them for Me (Ezekiel 33:7).

A Voice: She is a voice crying in the wilderness of life to many in this generation with the mandate to evangelize and prepare many for the coming of our Lord Jesus Christ...The voice of one crying in the wilderness, Prepare ye the way of the Lord, make his paths straight." (Matthew 3:3).

If you would like to invite Raeni Bankole as a teacher of the word at your seminar or church group program; please send an email to Nehemiahtroop@gmail.com.

Nehemiah Troop Prayer Ministry (NTPM)

...raising an army of intercessors

The Nehemiah Troop Prayer Ministry also known as "The Upper Room" is a weekly prayer school that has a mandate to raise fire-branded watchmen for the Kingdom of our Lord Jesus Christ. It follows after the vision of Nehemiah in the bible that didn't rest until he had rebuilt the walls of Jerusalem. He didn't do it alone; he had the king and his brethren (Nehemiah 2:1-20). Like Nehemiah, many of us today must be empowered to save our Father's house!

The vision of NTPM is to raise an army of intercessors all across the land and send out the clarion call for the prophet of nations to take their place on the prayer watches like Daniel who ushered their nation and generation into divine purpose.

There is a weekly phone conference every Saturday at 7:00 a.m. (CST) via freeconferencing.com: **Dial 641-715-1300 Access Code 328037.**

Our live meeting and healing school holds every last Saturday of the month at 12 noon in major hotels all across the United States of America.

For more details please view news and events at
www.empowermentmission.org or
the Nehemiah Troop page on Facebook.

Nehemiah Troop Scholarship Fund (NTSF)

...empowering lives through education

Nehemiah Troop Scholarship Fund (NTSF) is a branch of the Raeni Bankole ministry that empowers young people in the Diaspora through education. The vision was born out of a need to help international students schooling abroad pay their tuition. As the coordinator, Raeni Bankole experienced firsthand what most international students with limited resources go through in order to stay in school. She came to the United States in 2001 to earn a masters' degree but dropped out of the program after two semesters due to extreme financial hardship. It took over ten years to regain the dream of obtaining a masters' degree and the NTSF is a fulfillment of the vision to repair the breach and restore the path for many generations to dwell in.

The average cost of tuition per semester in the United States is $8000 - $10,000 and most international student cannot work outside the campus to support themselves. They usually have to drop out of school and defer the dream of furthering their education. It is extremely difficult to survive outside school because they also do not have employment authorization to make any living. Staying registered in school helps these young international students maintain F-1 status and achieve their academic dream. Please join us as we empower lives one day at a time through the Nehemiah Troop Scholarship Fund.

We want to hear from you!

Please send your comments about this book using the contact details below:

Phone: 630-936-8868
E-mail: nehemiahtroop@gmail.com
Website: www.empowermentmission.org

Please include your testimony of help received from this book when you write.
Your prayer requests are welcome.

You can order additional copies of this book or any other book by the author online @
www.amazon.com
or simply send us an email or call us.

Dewalette Creations

Are you an author?

Would you like to have your book published?

It would be our delight to review your manuscript in preparation for an outstanding publication.

CONTACT US:

Phone:
(630) 481-6305

Email:
dewalette@gmail.com
info@dewalette.com

www.ingramcontent.com/pod-product-compliance
Lightning Source LLC
LaVergne TN
LVHW051550070426
835507LV00021B/2501